Dismantling Injustice

Dismantling Injustice

A Disorderly Parable of the Song of Solomon

APRIL LOVE-FORDHAM

With a foreword by Catherine Meeks

Art by Kit Fordham

RESOURCE *Publications* · Eugene, Oregon

DISMANTLING INJUSTICE
A Disorderly Parable of the Song of Solomon

Disorderly Parable Bible Studies Series

Resource Publications
An Imprint of Wipf and Stock Publishers
199 W. 8th Ave., Suite 3
Eugene, OR 97401

www.wipfandstock.com

PAPERBACK ISBN: 978-1-4982-8913-9
HARDCOVER ISBN: 978-1-4982-8915-3
EBOOK ISBN: 978-1-4982-8914-6

Manufactured in the U.S.A.   05/20/16

Unless otherwise noted, all biblical quotations are taken from the Holy Bible, New Revised Standard Version (NRSV), copyright © 1991, 1994 Oxford University Press, Inc.

This book is dedicated to people everywhere who dismantle injustice with the one tool that can heal both victim and oppressor:
God's love.

To Steve, Brent, Kit, Chanelle, Sharon, and Becky who are numbered with those people.

To Maggie Mayhem, my Great Dane puppy, who was with me every stroke of the keyboard.

A cruel plantation owner is walking in the hot cotton field when he strides up to his slave, Hattie, who is picking cotton along with her eight-year-old son Cecil and husband Earl.

"Hattie, come on, I need your help in the shed," demands her slave master. Anger emanates from the slave master at Hattie's hesitation to go with him into the shed. He demands again, "Come on!" Hattie is visibly terrified. She unwillingly follows him into the shed.

Young Cecil, witnessing all of this and worried about his mother asks, "Pa, where is he taking Ma?"

His father, Earl, scared for both his wife and son, replies sternly, "Get back to work." Cecil refuses to listen and runs after his mother.

Earl screams, "Cecil come back here, boy!" Earl runs after Cecil and grabs hold of him. Cecil watches as the slave master takes Hattie into the shed. Sensing the danger his mother is in, he screams, "Mama!"

"Come here!" Earl pleads. "Look at me, boy! Don't you lose your temper with that man. This is his world. We're just living in it. You hear me? Now get on back to work."

—Interpretive notes from the opening scene of the movie,
Lee Daniels' The Butler (2014)

Contents

Foreword

Dismantling Injustice: A Disorderly Parable of the Song of Solomon brings the voices of a very rich array of characters from everyday life and the Holy Scriptures to the conversation of dismantling racism. This is a conversation that stands in dire need of new ways to be held. The old methods of years past are not adequate because there have been many changes in the landscape, but in spite of them, there are many ways that it has remained the same. The threads of racism that plagued the main character in this book, Congressman Caleb Morgan, in the early years of his life continue to thrive in America. They have become somewhat more sophisticated thus making it a bit harder to name them at times. But they are alive and well and all efforts to address them have to take their subtle nature into consideration. The racism of the twenty-first century has to be addressed amid the cries that America is now post racial. Of course all thoughtful and honest people know that it is not.

The election of President Obama has contributed more than anyone would have imagined to moving us closer to our racial truth. Some of the rage that is being vented in this present moment toward those in power is deeply rooted in the fear that is encompassing the hearts of those who thought that the presidency was for "white men only." For the past eight years, they have had to live with the daily challenge that is presented to that notion by the presence of an African-American in the White House. This daily dose of reality has become intolerable and we see how it is being acted out in our daily political life.

Along with this, we have seen white rage demonstrated by others as well. The most vivid examples are found in police behaviors in African American communities and in the ways that many policemen believe that they can treat nonwhite citizens. The highly publicized police shootings that we have witnessed are only a tip of the iceberg of rage and fear that is not as deeply submerged as it was in past years. But, the rage and fear can continue to remain nameless in conversations unless there are honest persons speaking with one another who truly seek to speak and hear the truth.

Dismantling Injustice helps the reader to see that the cycle can be broken when people are willing like the young Shulammite woman from the Song of Solomon to hold fast to a deep internal conviction to the Good Shepherd. Faith that generates the ability not to be compromised by the trappings of oppression can lead to dismantling injustice. This hopeful message is so timely in this era of a mass sense of hopelessness and the willingness to acquiesce to polarization and violence as a way to respond.

April Love-Fordham has brilliantly woven the story of Congressman Morgan and the story from the Song of Solomon into an engaging tapestry that invites the reader to travel on the path with the characters as well as engaging in personal reflection and spiritual practice. This is refreshing because it provides a very concrete way for the reader to make a response to the impact of *Dismantling Injustice* as each section is read.

As a fifty-year veteran in this work of seeking paths to racial healing, I am delighted to know that *Dismantling Injustice* will be available as a part of the toolkit for healing. We need all of the healing voices that we can find to help in this challenging work. I am thankful for April Love-Fordham's voice as it is presented in this powerful testament.

Catherine Meeks, PhD

Catherine Meeks is the retired Clara Carter Acree Distinguished Professor of Socio-Cultural Studies of Wesleyan College, the chair of the Beloved Community: the Commission for Dismantling Racism for the Episcopal Diocese of Atlanta, the author of five books, a religion columnist for Huffington Post, a community and wellness activist, and a mid-wife to the soul.

Preface

Every morning, until you are dead in the ground, you are going to have to make this decision . . . You are going to have to ask yourself, "Am I going to believe what them fools say about me today?" . . . All my life I'd been told what to believe about politics, coloreds, being a girl. But . . . I realized I actually had a choice in what I could believe."

—Aibileen Clark[1]

The Song of Solomon has a powerful message that has sometimes been twisted into appalling and simply absurd interpretations. One common interpretation compares God to King Solomon who kept sex slaves and benevolently seduced them (several hundred of them) into his bed. This interpretation claims that the relationship between the King and one of his sex slaves illustrated the perfect, intimate love between God and each of us. Another interpretation claims that the Song was an ancient sex manual—instructing married couples how to enjoy God-approved sex. To believe this version is to believe that the lust of the mighty King Solomon was sacred and that the oppressed—his many sex slaves—experienced complete sexual fulfillment in his arms. However, those versions are not the real story of the Song of Solomon. The real story is one of resisting and overcoming oppression while falling intimately in love with the Creator.

In reading this book, you will walk away with both a parable that will challenge you, and a thorough verse-by-verse understanding of the Song of Solomon. In addition, at the end of every section, there are instructions for a spiritual practice tailored to help those who practice it draw closer to God.

1. Stockett, *The Help*, 63.

The Parable

Jesus used parables—stories of everyday people—to illustrate spiritual truths. His parables were not nice, tidy stories. They were subversive and meant to challenge things that the listener thought were truth, but were not. *Dismantling Injustice: A Disorderly Parable of the Song of Solomon* is a story of everyday people that illustrates the spiritual truths found in the Song of Solomon. First, it will cause you to question everything you thought you knew about the Song. Second, it will teach you how to identify and oppose unjust world systems. Finally, it will demonstrate how the dismantling of unjust systems begins within your own heart.

Spiritual Practices

I am persuaded that each of us has a profound longing for God, but I am also convinced that God has an unfathomable longing for each of us. Despite our flaws, God sees us as beautiful and precious. Yet, God does not force God's love upon us. We can either allow God to draw near or push God away. The spiritual disciplines in this book give us an intentional way to open ourselves to God and experience the fullness of a relationship with God. Not coincidentally, as seen throughout Scripture, those who grow close to God are often empowered to dismantle injustice whether it is large-scale social injustice or seemingly small injustice in our own backyards. These spiritual practices can be transformative. I encourage you to give them a try.

Group Study

If you are studying this book with a group, then you may find Appendix 1 useful. Appendix 1 divides the book into eight lessons and offers questions that will jumpstart group discussions.

Disclaimer

This parable is a true story in the sense that it is a combination of embellished facts. All names, dates, places, events, and details have been changed, invented, and altered for literary effect. The reader should not consider this parable to be about any particular part of my life or any particular community of people. It is a work of literature.

Disorderly Parable Bible Studies

Dismantling Injustice: A Disorderly Parable of the Song of Solomon is the second book in the *Disorderly Parable Bible Studies* series. The first was *James in the Suburbs: A Disorderly Parable of the Epistle of James.*

Acknowledgments

I would gratefully like to acknowledge the following people who have played significant roles in the writing of this book:

Steve Fordham who is still the best husband ever. The fact that my books exist at all are because you have—without a single complaint—paid the bills while I studied, wrote about, and taught scripture. I love you!

Brent Fordham who spent considerable time lending me his expertise on the Song of Solomon, his editorial expertise, and his wholehearted support. You are a kind and amazing man.

Kit Fordham and Chanelle Gallagher who have been my inspiration. Not a visit or long telephone conversation goes by when you have not struggled with me over how injustice can be dismantled and oppressors overcome. You daily live out what others only talk about! Special thanks to Kit Fordham for his illustrations, which make this book complete. You can see more of his impressive work at artkit.co.

Sharon Fordham who has been an excellent editor and cheerleader. I am so grateful that you are also my sister-in-law. You continue to amaze me as you live into the call Christ has on your life.

Becky Mathews Beal who has once again done a wonderful job of editing and giving me advice. I am so blessed to know you and to have your help. Thank you from the bottom of my heart.

Willie Jones who read the first draft of my book in order to give me an intentional African-American perspective and who told me that I was definitely the person to write this story. You have been a good friend for many years.

The women who I had the honor of mentoring in my spiritual direction group. We prayed together an hour a day for nine months! Wow! You were all such a blessing to me: Sharon Gordon, Donna Nolfa, Elizabeth

Forsten, Sue Farner, Kay Anderson, Vonceal Kubler, Carol Keith, and Karen Wright. Thank you for sharing your lives with me.

The parishioners, clergy, and staff at Saint David's Episcopal Church. I have never known a more authentic gathering of believers. The blessings you have given Steve and me are beyond number. You have let us join with you in being the hands and feet of Jesus for our Unidad families. You have come to my classes and the events that I have led. Thank you!

Rev Dr. Kenneth Swanson and Rev Anne Elizabeth Swiedler who are the best priests, encouragers, and teachers I have ever known. I would still be going through life feeling alone had Father Swanson not taught me how and to pray. You gave me the gift of being able to find God in God's garden.[2]

The wonderful faculty and staff of Columbia Theological Seminary who invited me to campus to work on this book as a Guthrie Scholar. Special thanks to Rev Dr. Sarah F. Erickson, Mary Martha Riviere, Michael Thompson, Rev Dr. Israel Galindo, Rev Dr. Roger Nishioka, and Rev Dr. William Brown who in their various and wonderful ways enabled and inspired me to write this book.

The gracious Dr. Catherine Meeks, who wrote the foreword for this book. I am an admirer of the hard work you have done dismantling racism throughout your life. I also have great admiration of your work with the "Beloved Community: the Commission for Dismantling Racism" of the Episcopal Diocese of Atlanta. This group does an incredible job of helping us see God's face in everyone while "creating new paths upon which God's light and love can shine in ways that make us a beloved community."

The helpful and kind librarians of the Fulton County Library, who helped me get the materials I needed to do research—especially Karen Swenson, who not only tolerated my many requests and missing library cards, but was also a source of encouragement every time I saw her. To Becky Kennedy and Barbara White, I could not have written this book without the fifty or so interlibrary loans you obtained for me from parts unknown.

My parents, Charles and Mary Dorcas Love who have always encouraged me to be all God created me to be.

Wipf and Stock, especially Matthew Wimer, Brian Palmer, and James Stock who have been so very patient with my questions. I can't tell you how impressed I am with the Wipf and Stock staff and business model.

In memory of Rev Dr. Stephen Hayner, who wrote the foreword to *James in the Suburbs*. One Sunday after church long ago, you said to me,

2. Song 6:1–2.

"You are a good writer" referring to a paper I had written for you in seminary. My son heard you say it. I didn't think much about it, but when we got to the car, my son said, "The past President of Intervarsity Press just told you that you are a good writer. That has to be a sign, mom!" I miss you and your joyful inspiring faith.

Finally, in memory of Sophie, my ancient fifteen-year-old enormous black and white spotted Great Dane, who made a cameo appearance in *James in the Suburbs*. It broke my heart that you finally had to leave us. To Maggie Mayhem, my new gray mantle merle Great Dane puppy. You have big paws to fill, but what hilarious joy you have brought back to our house!

The Meet Cute

Now may the God of peace, who brought back from the dead our Lord Jesus, the great shepherd of the sheep, by the blood of the eternal covenant, make you complete in everything good so that you may do his will, working among us that which is pleasing in his sight, through Jesus Christ, to whom be the glory forever and ever. Amen.

—Hebrews 13:20–21

1

Surprised by the Holy Spirit

"Those who plan everything to a 'T' don't allow themselves to be surprised by the freshness, fantasy, and novelty of the Holy Spirit."

—Pope Francis[1]

It was the cold winter morning of February 26, 1998. I was late as usual. Despite my propensity to be organized and professional, I was almost always late. I would work on whatever project or hobby had captured my interest until I made myself *almost* late. Then I would rush off, panicked, desperate to still make the appointment on time. Even so, the fear of being late was minor compared to my fear of being bored. I hated standing around—or even sitting around, for that matter—with nothing to do. So I was doomed to rush from place to place often five minutes late. Or, let's be honest, sometimes fifteen. This morning was no different. Today, I was late for my flight back to DC.

I vowed silently that the next time would be different. I would leave early. I would find a hobby I could do while I waited. Then I would be late no more. But as I mentioned, this morning was no different than usual. Same vow as usual too. A vow that would soon be forgotten like all of the other identical vows made in the frustration of the moment.

Looking out the dirty window of my cab for the first time, I noticed that it was dark outside even though it was half past nine. The clouds in the sky were foreboding. Rain came down in torrents. It was cold outside, but

1. Pope Francis's address to the Curia on December 23, 2014.

3

not cold enough to snow. There were only a few cabs in front of mine at the terminal, but I was unwilling to wait for the taxi to reach the sheltered drop-off point. So I paid my fare, grabbed my briefcase and overnighter, and ran toward the terminal. Upon entering the terminal, soaking wet, my greatest fear was realized. The announcement scrolling across the bottom of the arrival-departure screen said that my flight was delayed. I was going to be bored for certain now. A six-hour delay! CNN, on a screen a few feet away, announced that temperatures were quickly dropping. The rain had already turned to snow in most cities. Snow was going to shut down the entire northeastern seaboard: New York, Philadelphia, Baltimore, and Washington, DC. Having already checked out of my hotel room, I was stuck.

Disgruntled, I went to my gate and looked for a seat next to a window. It wasn't hard to find. There was a mass of empty benches, each with five bucket seats, lined up perpendicular to the windows. At least I could watch the dark winter storm clouds roll across the sky as the rain turned to ice and eventually snow. I sighed, flung my belongings into the seat next to mine, and sat down. I was alone—not another soul anywhere near the gate—except for the woman staffing the coffee kiosk, which smelled of hot chocolate and apple cider in addition to coffee beans. Apparently, everyone else had had the foresight to check the weather before heading to the airport. Not I. I had worked out on a stair machine in the smelly hotel gym while watching reruns of C-SPAN testimony on allegations against President Clinton. Despite my present frame of mind, I had actually woken up in an exceptional mood. I was feeling a great deal of personal success having recently gotten a humorous op-ed piece published in the New York Times. It was written in support of the feminist non-profit group raising money for a defense fund for Monica Lewinsky. The piece had gotten a lot of mileage among my friends and co-workers. I was basking in my fifteen minutes of fame.

However, at that moment, sitting there in the empty terminal in the molded-plastic bucket seat, I was already bored. Because of government regulations, I only had a pad of yellow paper to doodle on. My state of the art IBM ThinkPad 380 laptop that I used in my day job contained classified government information and was being shipped back to my office along with the other materials I had used to make a presentation the previous day. Apparently, you could trust the post office with classified material, but not Delta. In reality, I could have brought my laptop with me on the plane, but only if I were willing to wear it handcuffed to my wrist—an inconvenient regulation at best. Just try navigating a plane's tiny, unkempt restroom with one wrist strapped to a laptop and see how well that works out.

I was silently lamenting my situation when it happened. It was no happy accident. It was better. It was an outstanding event, which I would treasure for a lifetime—one of those incredible happenings that sweetens as the years pass. I was to meet a man like none I had ever met before. We were unlikely friends. He was fifty-six years my senior. I was twenty-eight, white, and just beginning my career. He was eighty-four, black, and had just announced the end of his career. What brought us together were his bold grit and my dogged curiosity. Yet his implausible friendship would forever change the way I saw the world.

As I sat staring through the giant picture window at the ominous clouds moving together to form one massive blanket that would soon encompass the entire sky, he lumbered toward me from across the terminal. I glanced in his direction to see who had entered. He was a large man dressed in a dark blue suit, a starched white shirt, and a cobalt blue tie with matching suspenders. Very classy in an I-have-my-own-style way. The way he walked reminded me of an old superman—once able to leap tall buildings, but because of age, now limited to taking the stairs. Still in no way decrepit—he simply took the stairs, not the elevator. He was as fit as a man his age could be—just old. Another black man, my age, was with him. He was just as distinguished and carried himself with just as much a sense of dignity. The younger man was carrying a black leather briefcase and talking on a cell phone. The older man held nothing but a bottled water and a rolled up newspaper.

I glanced away quickly so as not to seem to notice them. Yet, they kept walking my way getting closer and closer. The closer they got, the more uncomfortable I felt. The terminal was quite large and still empty. Why didn't they give me some space and at least sit on the other side of the ticket booth? The younger man held back at the edge of the seating area to finish his phone call, but the older gentleman walked to the bench facing mine and claimed a seat directly across from me. He took off his suit jacket, hung it over the seat, and while still standing held out his hand, and said, "Good morning!"

With his enormous hand outstretched toward me, it was obviously impossible to pretend any longer that I hadn't noticed him. By reflex, I held out my hand, which looked childlike in comparison to his. To my complete surprise, as I looked up into his eyes, I recognized him. *The* United States

Congressman Caleb Morgan. His eyes had me—immediately. They were perhaps the kindest eyes I had ever seen. They were a light hazel color with sparks of gold. He had a graying goatee and short graying hair.

"Looks like we have a six hour wait," he announced. "My name is Caleb, but you know that," he chuckled—pleased with himself. "I saw the recognition cross your face when we shook hands!" He was not trying to hide the fact that he liked being recognized. It amused him.

"Yes sir. It would be hard not to recognize you. I'm a big fan."

I started to tell him my name, but before I could, he asked, "What do you do for a living?"

"Congressman Morgan, I can't tell you that." My response was sassy and playful.

"My goodness woman! Why not?"

"You'll stop talking to me." Our eyes locked and he thought about it. I didn't realize it at the time, but he was the one playing me.

"You are a reporter?" he guessed.

"No. I'm a technology advisor to the White House. I work for a DC think-tank."

Again, he laughed. "I know you who are."

"You know me?" Now I was genuinely confused.

"I was in the room yesterday when you gave status to the Joint Chiefs. Good move your firm made when they sent *you* to give the status. Never seen the chiefs be so gentle on the bearer of bad news during a Q&A session before."

I was still beyond words that this important man was speaking to me. And even more stunned that he knew me. By no means was I anyone important. The meeting to which he referred had been a crowded gathering of sixty or so. Most were in uniform. I had only been allowed in the oversized meeting room during my presentation. Then I was escorted to a dull waiting room, with no windows, white walls, and speckled floor tiles. I was to remain there available in case there were any questions for me later. However, Congressman Morgan was right. My boss had sent me to deliver the status because he thought the powers that be would go easy on me. Overwhelmed, I sat, eyes wide, and staring at Congressman Morgan with no reply.

The silence lasted a bit too long. He let the thought that I had been stalked settle into my head. After a second, he went on, "There is *no* reason that I can't talk to you, young lady. I see you have a pad of paper and a pen.

We have work to do. Six hours until the plane departs. I think that is just about enough time."

"How is that?"

He was lighthearted and teasing me, but I sensed there was something he wanted from me. I wondered where this was going to take us. "Are we going to be doing espionage together, Congressman Morgan?"

"I have a story for you to write."

"I'm not a writer."

"I beg to differ. Yesterday, I saw you weave an otherwise lackluster status report into an irresistible story. The chiefs listened. You are a natural storyteller. Plus everyone has read your op-ed on the Lewinsky affair."

"I don't think *everyone* has read it." I smiled proudly.

He shook his head knowingly and laughed, "I have been looking for a woman to write my story for me. I have talked to several writers. It's too religious and touchy feely for most. They don't get it and I don't want them to write it. However, you have the raw skills that I'm looking for: freshness and a sly sense of humor. I realized it yesterday while I was listening to you speak. Then when I saw you get out of the cab this morning, I considered it a divinely planned encounter. Too old to chase you down, I realized we were probably both on the same plane back to DC and decided to catch up with you on the plane and make you a proposal you'd be crazy to refuse. But this is outstanding—a six hour delay."

His request didn't just seem preposterous. It was preposterous! I didn't know if I could write. I did know that I already had a job that kept me busy fourteen hours a day, six days a week. But he was so important and so certain that our encounter was of a divine nature that I didn't dare argue. Besides, if I refused, it wouldn't have been because I was too busy, it would have been because I was too afraid of disappointing him.

He leaned forward and took a very serious tone, "Do you believe in God?"

"I do. But I rarely go to church. I got turned off while I was in college by the lack of women in leadership positions. I'm one of those people who likes the teachings of Jesus, but I'm not so hot on his present day followers."

"Perfect. Have you read the Bible?"

"Except for all of the 'begots.'"

"So and so begotten by so and so?" he questioned.

"Exactly."

"They are a bit tedious," he conceded.

"I did take some elective Bible courses in college and I've written an article for a Christian feminist magazine too. Why do you ask?"

"Because my story weaves together my life and a Bible story—a Bible story that changed my entire life—a Bible story that has sadly been misinterpreted by the great majority of scholars."

He paused and I stared into his beautiful old eyes. The moment felt holy. Holy was a feeling I was unfamiliar with and immediately wanted to shake off. It scared me a bit. But I plowed through it.

"So you think that I, a lowly staffer, who writes controversial op-eds in her free time, am qualified to interpret the Scripture while weaving your story into it?"

"My father was a minister. He has done the exegeting for us. I will teach you what he taught me and I will tell you my story. All you have to do is the weaving."

"What is your goal for this project?"

"In my opinion, a good deal of the church is unhealthy. It teaches theology, morality, and, occasionally, good works. But it doesn't teach people enough about having a relationship with God. Hence, the church—and churchgoers—have morphed into something virtually unrecognizable as belonging to Christ. Instead of using our intimate, life-changing relationship with God to put God's healing love into action, too often the church ignores who God is and where God is leading them. When this happens, the church has been known to participate in racism, sexism, and many other injustices instead of being the hands and feet of Christ."

Then he wagged his finger at me, "You've had a taste of that unhealthiness and the unhealthiness is exactly why you left the church."

He was right. "Why do you want a woman to write it?"

"Because it has a strong woman character and is immensely applicable to the women's movement. A man is never going to do that aspect justice. But you can. Any woman who has the guts to show compassion to Monica Lewinsky has the guts to think out of the box about right and wrong."

Now I was beyond intrigued. Thrilled really. Plus I wasn't going to have to spend the next six hours in the airport bored. I was ready to listen.

8

2
_____

The Shulammite

"Gimme hate, Lord," he whimpered. "I'll take hate any day. But don't give me love. I can't take no more love, Lord. I can't carry it . . . It's too heavy. Jesus, you know, you know all about it. Ain't it heavy? Jesus? Ain't love heavy?"

—Henry Porter[1]

"I was the Shulammite." Those were the words that Congressman Morgan, or Caleb, as I would come to call him, used to start his story. He said them as a declaration of truth as if they summed up who he was in his entirety. I had no clue what a Shulammite was, but when he didn't take a breath for me to slip in a question, I jotted it down on my yellow notepad for later.

His story took me way back in time to February 1968, two years before I was even born, to the Monday morning of his first week as the new baseball coach at Grandville High School. It was a big county high school about forty minutes west of Atlanta with a brand spanking new all-brick athletic facility. Segregation had just been made illegal and that had opened the door for this opportunity. Most all-white high school doors were still closed to black teachers, but Grandville coveted Caleb's consistently winning baseball teams. So even though the school was 98 percent white and characteristically racist with an active chapter of the KKK meeting there every other month, they hired him. He would be the only black teacher.

1. Morrison, *Song of Solomon*, 24.

9

Still, he was looking forward to starting over.

So far, his life felt like a lot of "starting overs." He had started over when his precious grandmother, the only family he had ever known, had died. Reverend Morgan (better known as "Doc" to his African-American congregants who spanned all of Colquitt County) and Reverend Morgan's wife had adopted Caleb at ten years of age. He had started over when at twenty-five he got a full scholarship to Jackson State to play football. He had started over again when he was drafted by the Browns into the All-American Football Conference.

Up until then, starting over had always meant moving to something bigger and better than what he had previously had. Well, maybe not better—his tiny, bent over, wrinkled, old grandmother with flashing brown eyes had been the absolute best and always would be even though his adopted parents, the Morgans, took a close second. But moving in with them, meant he no longer worried where his next meal might come from or if he and his grandmother would have enough money for heat in the few weeks of winter that they experienced in the Deep South. If not exactly better, the moves were always definitely bigger. To bigger houses, more money, richer successes.

However, that run of "bigger and better" had changed five years into playing for the Browns. He heard a crack in his neck during practice. The C-5 vertebra in his neck cracked upon impact. It simply seemed dizzying at first. But within seconds, he lost control of his legs. Starting over that time, it seemed that bigger and better was not a possibility. Unemployed and essentially homeless, it was a year before he could walk again and another year before he regained his strength. Even then, he would never play football again.

After a fairly short battle with depression, he realized that all was not lost. He married his high school sweetheart and landed a coaching job back in his hometown in the run down all-black high school where he had grown up. But he wasn't coaching football. They had needed a baseball coach and felt he could handle it. He needed a job. Twelve good years had followed and he had grown to like baseball even better than football. His all-black teams had done phenomenally well and a few of his boys had gone on to play in college.

Then his spirited, perfect-in-every-way, wife died of breast cancer. He was devastated.

It was at that juncture that the low pay, the one horse town where he had lived all of his life, and the dealing with the same old problems sprouting from students swallowed up in poverty began to overwhelm him.

So, here he was. He was starting over again.

But this time, he was on his own—for the first time in his life no external circumstances were pushing him on down the road. This time it was coming from inside. He was angry, tired, and restless. This time he was taking matters into his own hands.

He didn't want to feel the love he had once felt for his community any longer. It was too much for him. Too painful. He could never feel hate for his community, but he just didn't want to feel love any more. He wanted to go somewhere where he felt nothing for a change.

The civil rights movement was in full swing. He and his community were well aware that they were caught in an unjust system that they had not chosen. These once victims of slavery were now victims of inhumane poverty, underpaid even when they were able to get work outside of picking cotton. Segregation was a tightly held unjust system, which had even kept his wife from getting proper medical care. The white hospital wouldn't let her in the door. The "Negro hospital"—in a medical building too run down for the white folks to go to any longer—was half a day's bus ride away sitting the entire way in the back (of course) of an unpleasant, neglected bus. During her visits, if she was lucky enough to get a room, she shared it with five or six other very sick women.

The less than modern medical care she had gotten had left him broke. After her death, he had grown more and more resolved to escape from all of the things that held a black man back. He had even convinced his father and the church elders that they needed to go with him to Selma where they marched with Martin Luther King Jr. and others. Caleb wanted change and it couldn't come soon enough. He wanted success, a nice house, a nice car, and proper health care. But after witnessing the chaos and violence in Selma, it became evident to him that he could not arrange for every black man to have the things he might be able to get for himself. That was his downfall. The day he fell in love with the idea of having fancy things for himself without regard to the needs of his brothers.

So this was another day of starting over. This time, it was with no one's interest in mind but his own. He felt great—convinced that he had won the jackpot.

The tall, yet unattractive, athletic director at his new school, a man whose main goal in life was to keep the fans just happy enough to let him keep his job, was to be out of town the morning Caleb started. Therefore, Sunday afternoon they had met in the sunny tree lined parking lot to exchange the keys he would need. That is how Caleb gained entry the next morning and was able to surprise the boys huddled in the spotless locker room, which still smelled of new paint.

Caleb had been wandering through the facility with a big smile on his face taking it all in when he heard voices coming from the locker room. The door had been left propped open with a trashcan so he entered without a sound. A transaction of amphetamines was underway. Caleb stood out of the boys' line of sight and listened. They hadn't noticed him, but he could see them in a mirror that was hanging on the back of a locker across the room. The largest of the three boys—a white boy Caleb would later learn was considered the team's ace—was selling the drug to the other two younger players. One of them was a black student who had been recruited from the nearby black high school to increase the chances of a state championship.

From the conversation, the younger white boy had obviously doped before, but not the black guy. The ace had gotten the drugs for the younger guys. Caleb stood motionless, waiting to see what would happen. After the money had traded hands, the ace gave instructions to the black boy on how to inject the amphetamines.

"Show me," insisted the black player as he exposed his bicep.

As the ace showed the boy how to prepare the syringe, Caleb rounded the corner. The boys didn't move. Caleb was blocking the entrance to the locker room, but not the exit. They didn't know Caleb from Adam, but they were conspicuously unconcerned that Caleb saw them. The ace placed the syringe in the box he had delivered the drugs in, put it on the bench, shook the hands of the two younger players, and started walking toward the exit. The black player gathered up the goods and stuck them in his locker.

Lowering his voice an octave and standing a half inch taller, Caleb demanded, "Where do you think you're going?" The ace glanced back, but kept walking. "Stop!" demanded Caleb to no avail.

Caleb turned his attention to the younger players. "Give me the box."

"Are you serious?" asked the remaining white player.

"Damn right I'm serious."

"Who the hell are you?"

"I'm the new coach. And no one on my team dopes. Give me the box."

The black kid handed him the box and the two boys started to follow the ace out the exit.

"Sit down." Caleb demanded. But no one sat down. They kept walking. They exhibited no fear. Caleb was just an irritant to them—a gnat that would be squashed if it came too close. Knowing the boys couldn't get far and that he had possession of the drug, he let them go. After all, it was his first day and his only other choice was to take physical action against them. He looked back at the locker that the ace had been using. Last names had been painted in block letters on the metal doors. His was Bennett.

∗∗∗

Back at the airport, the rain turned to snow. Congressman Morgan's assistant walked over and whispered something in his ear while holding up a message pad so the congressman could read what was written on it. As soon as Congressman Morgan answered, his good-looking assistant gave me a friendly smile. I smiled back, but the assistant was gone almost immediately. He had taken a seat out of earshot of our conversation and appeared to be busy working.

I took this pause in Congressman Morgan's story to ask my first question, "You said you were the Shulammite? What does that mean?"

"Well, the Shulammite is the young heroine of an ancient Old Testament love story—a sort of primitive opera.[2] It's sometimes called the Song of Songs and sometimes the Song of Solomon. The heroine's name is never told, but in a later act of the opera, she is called the Shulammite."[3]

Given Congressman Morgan's explanation, I was still having trouble seeing this big masculine man as a young Shulammite woman. But he rejected my further questions telling me with a twinkle in his eye to "listen

---

2. Ginsburg, *The Song of Songs*, 176–177 and Pope, *Song of Songs*, 596–600. There are many theories among scholars about the name or title "Shulammite." Ginsburg believed it was a title used to identify the heroine as being from the town of Shulem, now known as Sulam in northern Israel. Pope points out several other theories. Perhaps her name, being similar to Solomon, was meant to make the reader see her as an anti-Solomon or even a female Solomon. Could the ancient composer have given her a name that was simpatico with Solomon's—similar to Jack and Jill? Some have noticed that the name is similar to *shalom*, the Hebrew word for peace. They speculate that the author wished to emphasize what the Shulammite says about herself in Song 8:10: "I was in his eyes as one who brings peace."

3. Song 6:13.

up." To my satisfaction, the hours flew by and soon enough we were on a plane home. Congressman Morgan was in first class—forced there from his economy seat by an admiring flight crew. His assistant and I were in coach separated by several rows. Most importantly, we had a date when the three of us would meet to start the real work of organizing his story.

Relationship Assessment

When the narrator asked Caleb about the goal for the story, he replied, "In my opinion, a good deal of the church is unhealthy. It teaches theology, morality, and, occasionally, good works. But it doesn't teach people enough about having a relationship with God." Caleb's words should challenge us to think about our own spirituality. Do we have a connection with God? Does this relationship inform our lives? The goal of this Relationship Assessment is to meditate while asking God questions that look back at important times in our lives.

Ancient Judeo-Christian meditation differs in a few significant ways from more modern forms of meditation. For instance, the goal of the ancient practitioner was not to empty the mind, but to fill it with intentional focused thoughts about a particular subject—all the while letting the Holy Spirit speak into these thoughts. The ancient practitioner sought a place of quiet solitude in which to meditate, but they did not attempt to enter into a state of relaxation. Meditation was hard work. The Hebrew words for meditation literally mean to growl, groan, sigh, mutter, or speak. Figuratively, they mean to occupy oneself, ponder, imagine, and study. Try thinking of whatever the subject you are meditating on as a big plot of land that you would like to cultivate. Your job is to present this plot of land to God by describing what you know of it to God. As you describe it, you try to see it through God's eyes. Then, most importantly, you stop and let the Holy Spirit speak through your free flowing thoughts. As you enter this ultimate place of listening, picture God plowing up the plot of land you have presented—revealing what lies beneath the soil, removing rocks and obstacles to your clear understanding of the subject.

How to pray the Relationship Assessment

Day 1

Ask God to help you pick out four significant periods of your life to review. Name each of these times and give them a date range. Examples might be College Years (2000–4), Parents' Divorce (1984–86), or Illness and Death of a Friend (2012–13). They do not have to be consecutive periods in your life.

Days 1–4

Each day meditate on one of these periods of your life asking God to show you how your relationship with God during this time was strong or weak, why the relationship was strong or weak, and then journal what God reveals to you.

Day 5

Look back over your journal for the week. Ask God to show you what is common and different during the times that you were close to and far from God. Do any patterns emerge? What do you learn from these patterns?

Conflicting Interpretations

The LORD is my shepherd, I shall not want. He makes me lie down in green pastures; he leads me beside still waters; he restores my soul. He leads me in right paths for his name's sake. Even though I walk through the darkest valley, I fear no evil; for you are with me; your rod and your staff—they comfort me. You prepare a table before me in the presence of my enemies; you anoint my head with oil; my cup overflows. Surely goodness and mercy shall follow me all the days of my life, and I shall dwell in the house of the LORD my whole life long.

—Psalm 23:1–6

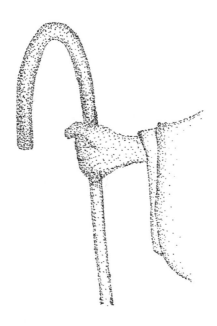

3
———

An Ancient Opera

Song 1:1

The Song of Songs, which is Solomon's.

—Song of Solomon 1:1

***

I woke up to sunshine flickering off of snow-covered streets the Saturday morning after my encounter with Congressman Morgan. After a breakfast of warm oatmeal topped with blueberries, I decided to put on my faux fur-lined boots and make my way to the esteemed Georgetown University Library, where faithful Jesuits had housed a treasure-trove of documents on the subject of the Shulammite. It was a windy, but beautiful fifteen-minute walk from the tiny English basement apartment I rented in a white brick townhouse in Georgetown. Finding a cozy, overstuffed chair, I settled in to explore the books that I had pulled from the dustless mahogany shelves.

The Song of Solomon, to which Congressman Morgan had referred, was an Old Testament book written a thousand or so years before the birth of Christ. Though today it is spoken of as a "book," it was likely performed as a sort of ancient opera on village greens.[1] Some scholars claimed that the first verse makes clear that the words were written by King Solomon him-

1. Smith, "Song of Solomon: The Shulammite and the King," disc 1.

19

self, while others say it was only *about* him, not *by* him. Some believed it was a fictional story written about the King, others believed it was a historical account. Either way, King Solomon was the King of Israel and son of King David. King David was the slayer of Goliath, writer of poetry, composer of songs, adulterer, murderer, and somehow, despite his sins, repented and became, once again, a man after God's own heart.[2] His son, King Solomon, had big shoes to fill with a demanding mission of his own—the building of the temple in Jerusalem.

It made sense that the Song was written by King Solomon, who was said in other Scripture to be a prolific songwriter like his dad.[3] Evidently, in those days, the manly thing to do when you weren't engaged in battle was to write songs. In this case, a love story about oneself. Interestingly, "The Song of Songs" was titled as though it was considered King Solomon's very best song.[4] Another work signed by King Solomon is Ecclesiastes, which, unbeknownst to me at the time, would become important later on in Congressman Morgan's story. It too begins in a similar fashion: "Vanity of vanities."[5] It makes one think that whatever King Solomon wrote or composed, he thought in extremes.

On the other hand, if King Solomon did not write the Song, something interesting emerges. The Song may have originated in the Northern Kingdom.[6] Its purpose may have been to encourage the Northern Kingdom to resist King Solomon.[7] Solomon's Northern Kingdom had deteriorated so badly during his reign due to forced labor and taxation that he was indeed a very unpopular king.[8] If so, the Northern Kingdom surely heard a message in the Song linking their struggle against Solomon with that of the Shulammite's struggle against Solomon. The song would have been a rallying cry for the Northern Kingdom, who were debating the possibility of secession. The Song called the people to draw close to God in order to overcome Solomon's oppression. In other words, if a young country girl

---

2. Acts 13:22.

3. 1 Kgs 4:32 states that King Solomon's "songs numbered a thousand and five."

4. Song 1:1.

5. Eccl 1:2. "Vanity of vanities" can also be translated as "Meaninglessness! Utter meaninglessness!"

6. Bullock, *An Introduction to the Old Testament Poetic Books*, 263–64.

7. Ibid., 254–59.

8. 1 Kgs 12:4.

from the Northern Kingdom could resist Solomon's unjust harem, then they could resist his unjust rule too.

To my amazement, as I perused book after book, I found that there were as many different theories about the Song as there were books interpreting it. Some more recent scholars believed it was an ancient manual illustrating God's ideal for love, sex, and marriage.[9] Still others believed that it was a collection of unrelated drinking songs sung for their pornographic entertainment—or taking that line of thinking down a notch, others saw it as a series of erotic Hebrew poetry.[10]

The ancient Jews, early church theologians, and early Christian mystics interpreted the book allegorically—as an expression of the intimate covenant relationship between God and humanity.[11] In it, they saw King Solomon as the god figure and the Shulammite as the covenant people (if they were Jewish) or the church (if they were Christian).[12] They saw a wedding day and a honeymoon, which represented the intimate committed relationship between humanity and God.

However, Solomon, at the writing of the Song, had more than sixty wives and eighty concubines.[13] In an Old Testament book, 1 Kings, generally believed to have been written five hundred years after the Song of Solomon, it is said that King Solomon's harem grew even larger reaching seven hundred wives and three hundred concubines.[14] The Shulammite was most certainly one of these concubines.[15] Concubines were used by the king for

9. Glickman, *A Song for Lovers.*

10. Falk, *The Song of Songs.*

11. Guyon, *Song of Songs of Solomon.*

12. Johnson, *Proverbs*, 130. Early rabbis drew on the motif of human marriage that had been developed by the prophets (including Hosea and Jeremiah) as symbolizing the covenant between God and humanity. Later Christians (Origen and Augustine) saw the book as an allegory of Christ and his bride, the church.

13. Song 6:8.

14. 1 Kgs 11:3.

15. Ginsburg, *The Song of Songs*, 16–17 and Copan, *Is God a Moral Monster?*, 110–12. Ginsburg points out that because the Shulammite was a peasant woman who has worked in the fields (Song 1:5–6) and was kidnapped by Solomon's men (Song 6:11–12), it is not possible that she has the pedigree to be Solomon's wife. Many scholars, such as Copan, often in order to justify the Song as a love story between Solomon and his concubine, have reasoned that wives and concubines were both treated very well in ancient Israel. However, Ginsburg writes that concubines were often given as gifts or outright captured. They were kept for the gratification of the man's carnal desires and were placed in the most inaccessible part of the palace where dogs or eunuchs guarded them. They were not

sex. Essentially that was their only purpose. This is hardly a legitimate setting for a divine love story. In truth, King Solomon was a slave master, who, in all likelihood, knew a lot about lust, but very little about meaningful male-female relationships. His keeping of sex slaves—and the capturing of the Shulammite[16]—showed little understanding of what it meant to truly love and respect the opposite sex. In addition, there was no way he could possibly meet either the emotional or the sexual needs of a harem that would eventually grow to a thousand women.

Given all of this, some scholars came to see the "Solomon as a picture of God" interpretation of the Song as highly problematic and even offensive.[17] Congressman Morgan and his father fell into this camp. Solomon was not a man who could (or should) represent the love of God for humanity or God's ideal for a perfect sex life. Nor did it seem likely to them that God would want God's followers to identify as sex slaves in the harem of God. For all of these reasons, some scholars came to reject the notion that Solomon represented God and that the Shulammite represented humanity. I agreed with them.

Fortunately, as early as the twelfth century, a theory developed which explained the Song in a way that addressed these concerns. It is often called "The Two Male Theory."[18] Scholar S.R. Driver, writing at the turn of the twentieth century noted that the two male theory had previously been "accepted by the majority of modern critics and commentators."[19] However, something happened to push this theory underground.

While taking a break from my research in the library, I walked outside and down the library stairs where I could peer out at the Potomac covered with patches of ice and snow. It was here that a thought occurred to me. I could not prove it, but I wondered if the two male theory hadn't been pushed underground in the last half of the 19th century so that the "God as a

---

allowed to leave the palace unguarded. Nor were they allowed visitors except for their closest family members. Their offspring were considered illegitimate heirs that were routinely barred from inheriting the father's title or estates, even when there was an absence of any legitimate heirs.

16. Song 6:12.

17. Ginsburg, *Song of Songs*, 20–102 and Kuak, *Song of Solomon*, 2–9.

18. Some examples of scholars who subscribe to the Two Male Theory include: Ibn Ezra in the twelfth century, J. Jacobi in 1771, S. Lowisohn in 1816, S. Lowisohn in 1826, Christian Ginsburg in 1857, Frederic Godet in 1894, S.R. Driver in 1913, John Patterson in 1932, Leroy Waterman in 1948, Hassell Bullock in 1988, and Iain Provan in 2001.

19. S. R. Driver, *An Introduction to the Literature of the Old Testament*, 437.

slave master" interpretation of the book could be used to justify first slavery and later racism. It would be a thought I would return to again and again as Congressman Morgan's story unfolded before me.

Congressman Morgan's father was known as Doc to the group of African-American churches that he pastored, but he wasn't a medical doctor. He had received a PhD in theology from Oberlin College. One thing he wanted his congregants to know was the Bible. He taught them well. Moreover, one thing that he taught them was the two male theory of the Song of Solomon. It would not be going too far to say that Doc's congregants, as well as Congressman Morgan, had adopted this interpretation as a lifelong guide for both developing a strong relationship with God and for dismantling injustice.

In Doc's interpretation, King Solomon, the powerful, lustful king that he was, has had his soldiers entice the Shulammite away from her community—her family, friends, and her beloved Shepherd (the second male in the story). This was perfectly legitimate in keeping with the original text, because the ancient Hebrew, while revealing the gender of characters, does not differentiate as to how many male characters are in the story. Doc, like the nineteenth-century scholar Ginsburg, distinguished between the lyrics attributed to the Shepherd by the use of pastoral language and the lyrics attributed to King Solomon by express allusions to his kingship.[20] The scholar S.R. Driver further differentiated between the two male characters by saying that "the speeches attributed to the king are somewhat stiff and formal," while those of the Shepherd, "breathe a warm and devoted affection."[21] Taking these aspects of the original text into consideration, the text allows for two main male characters both competing for the Shulammite's attention. One of the males is King Solomon, but, in Doc's interpretation, Solomon did not represent God. Instead, he was the lustful oppressor who desired the Shulammite for selfish reasons without regard for her well-being. It is the other male character, who the Shulammite calls "Beloved" and is referred to as "the Shepherd," who represents God. The Shepherd truly loves the Shulammite and is utterly selfless in his love for her.

In the two male theory, God is the Good Shepherd who seeks to free the Shulammite. This view of God as the Good Shepherd, who seeks out lost sheep, is consistent with many metaphors and parables of the Old and New Testament. The Shepherd pursues the Shulammite along with King

20. Ginsburg, *The Song of Songs*, 6–7.

21. S. R. Driver, *An Introduction to the Literature of the Old Testament*, 437.

23

Solomon, but he truly loves her, unlike the king. This love triangle demonstrates the struggle of the young Shulammite. One male, the oppressor, Solomon, has enslaved her in order to have his way with her. He is ready to please her—at least until he has conquered her. Of course, once he had conquered her, he would have certainly cast her aside along with the others in his ever-growing harem. The other male, the Shepherd, the God character, was her true love and passion, her savior and hero who put her interests before his own.

Doc's interpretation is of the Shulammite's struggle between Solomon and her beloved Shepherd. She can accept that her worth is found in being the king's sex slave. Or she can lean into her beloved Shepherd where she has infinite worth and is free to be all she was created to be. Will she succumb to the oppressor's unjust system, which enslaves her, or will she let her Shepherd rescue her and carry her home where she can be her best self? It is the relationship between the Shepherd and the Shulammite, not Solomon and the Shulammite, that illustrates the relationship between Christ and the church.[22] I saw this two male theory as ringing with great truth. I could not help but believe that Caleb's interpretation was not only as respectable as any other, but also probably the correct one. This interpretation was transformative and had the potential to change the world because it gave the oppressed a choice. The oppressed could continue being enslaved by Solomon who represented corrupt world powers—unjust world systems—or they could choose to run to their Creator's arms where they would be loved and nurtured.

I went back inside the library to gather my things and try to get warm before trekking toward home. A picture window near my chair provided a view from a higher elevation. From here, I could see over the Potomac with the Arlington Cemetery in the distance. The sun was starting to go down and the city glistened.

I thought about how Congressman Morgan had said that the Song had taught him how to dismantle oppression by drawing close to God. Though I did not yet know Congressman Morgan's entire story nor what he even meant by "drawing close to God," I did know that he had accomplished a magnitude in his twenty years as a congressional representative. He had worked on behalf of the oppressed creating opportunities that would allow them to succeed.

22. John 3:29, Eph 5:25–37, Rev 21:2, 10.

That day in the airport, there had been something beautiful shining out from Congressman Morgan's eyes—something numinous. It made me feel comfortable. But now, sitting there alone, staring through the picture window, I was completely terrified. I was terrified that his story might be too important for someone like me—someone with no real journalistic credentials whatsoever—to write. Yet, I was thrilled to the point of not being able to eat or sleep. We had planned to meet the following day at his Washington office.

4

Caleb's Interpretation
The Text of the Song of Solomon

One thing that makes the Song of Solomon so difficult to understand is that this ancient opera is all dialogue with no stage directions of any kind. However, even though there are no stage directions in the original Hebrew, many Bibles have found that they are helpful in giving the Song structure and context. Because of this, most Bibles have added some stage directions, usually in italics, in between chapters of the Song.

Some of these stage directions are as simple as indicating whether a male, female, or group is speaking. This is helpful, but these Bibles generally assume that there is only one male, one female, and one group (usually the harem) throughout the entire Song. These Bibles completely overlook the possibility that there may have been multiple men, women, and even groups with dialogue in the Song.

Stage directions in other Bibles are more complex, dividing the original text into acts and scenes, adding their best guess as to each scene's location. This can also be very helpful in understanding the story line too; however, they are often skewed to the "Solomon as a picture of God" theory. No matter how you understand the meaning of the story, adding stage directions is not an easy task, especially since this Song is the only drama of its type ever discovered in ancient Hebrew literature, and therefore there is nothing with which to compare and contrast it.[1]

---

1. Waterman, *The Song of Songs*, 3.

As I worked with Congressman Morgan and began to understand the Song of Solomon as his father had taught it to him, I began to annotate the New Revised Standard Version of the Song with stage directions that aligned specifically with Doc's interpretation of the Song. You will find my annotations—my stage directions—on the pages that follow. The New Revised Standard Version is in bold font. As you read these pages, you will notice that the dialogue, unaltered from the New Revised Standard Version of the Bible, has many nuances and curiosities that will be explained in later chapters of this book as Congressman Morgan's story is developed and the text is dissected section by section.

TITLE: 1:1 The Song of Solomon, which is Solomon's

Cast of Characters

Shulammite: A young peasant woman from the city of Shulem

King Solomon: The lustful King of Israel and adult son of King David

The Shepherd: A lowly male peasant from the city of Shulem who loves the Shulammite

Harem: Wives and concubines of King Solomon sometimes called Daughters of Jerusalem

Eunuchs: The castrated soldiers who guard the King's harem

Villagers: The villagers of Shulem in Solomon's Northern Kingdom

Girl: A young girl from the village of Shulem who is brought to the Shulammite for advice at the very end of the Song

Act 1: The Palace in Jerusalem

Scene 1: The Harem

SETTING: The chambers of KING SOLOMON's HAREM within his palace in Jerusalem.

AT RISE: KING SOLOMON enters the chambers of the HAREM to pick out his lover for the day.

HAREM

(The concubines of the HAREM long to be chosen by KING SOLOMON. Upon seeing KING SOLOMON, the HAREM whispers to one another excitedly.)

1:2 Let him kiss me with the kisses of his mouth!

(To get KING SOLOMON to notice them, they begin calling out to him.)

For your love is better than wine, 1:3 your anointing oils are fragrant, your name is perfume poured out;

EUNUCHS

(The EUNUCHS flatter KING SOLOMON.)

Therefore, the maidens love you.

SHULAMMITE

(The SHULAMMITE is new in the HAREM. She huddles in the corner alone. She doesn't want to be KING SOLOMON's lover. We hear her desperately cry out to her absent SHEPHERD to rescue her.)

1:4 Draw me after you, let us make haste. The king has brought me into his chambers.

HAREM

(The HAREM ignores her cries and calls to KING SOLOMON again.)

We will exult and rejoice in you; we will extol your love more than wine;

EUNUCHS

(The EUNUCHS flatter the King again.)

Rightly do they love you.

(KING SOLOMON picks the SHULAMMITE to be his lover for the day and leaves the chamber alone. The EUNUCHS stay to ensure that the SHULAMMITE will be presentable for KING SOLOMON.)

SHULAMMITE

(The SHULAMMITE begins to change to go meet with KING SOLOMON for the first time. The SHULAMMITE responds to the way the HAREM looks at her.)

1:5 **I am black and beautiful, O daughters of Jerusalem, like the tents of Kedar, like the curtains of Solomon.** 1:6 **Do not gaze at me because I am dark, because the sun has gazed on me. My mother's sons were angry with me; they made me keeper of the vineyards, but my own vineyard I have not kept!**

(Turning from the HAREM, she cries for her absent SHEPHERD again.)

1:7 **Tell me, you whom my soul loves, where you pasture your flock, where you make it lie down at noon; for why should I be like one who is veiled beside the flocks of your companions?**

HAREM

(The HAREM sarcastically tells her how to find her SHEPHERD.)

1:8 **If you do not know, O fairest among women, follow the tracks of the flock, and pasture your kids beside the shepherds' tents.**

Act 2: Solomon, The Oppressor

Scene 1: Solomon's Bedroom

SETTING: KING SOLOMON's luxurious bedroom suite inside his palace in Jerusalem. The EUNUCHS responsible for the concubines have made certain that the SHULAMMITE has been appropriately bathed, perfumed, dressed, and decorated with jewelry for her first meeting with KING SOLOMON.

AT RISE: KING SOLOMON is sitting on his ornate couch. The EUNUCHS bring the SHULAMMITE in.

KING SOLOMON

[1:9] I compare you, my love, to a mare among Pharaoh's chariots. [1:10] Your cheeks are comely with ornaments, your neck with strings of jewels. [1:11] We will make you ornaments of gold, studded with silver.

SHULAMMITE

(The SHULAMMITE speaks to her beloved SHEPHERD as if he were in the room.)

[1:12] While the king was on his couch, my nard gave forth its fragrance. [1:13] My beloved is to me a bag of myrrh that lies between my breasts. [1:14] My beloved is to me a cluster of henna blossoms in the vineyards of En-gedi.

KING SOLOMON

[1:15] Ah, you are beautiful, my love; ah, you are beautiful; your eyes are doves.

SHULAMMITE

(The SHULAMMITE continues to ignore KING SOLOMON and resumes talking to her absent SHEPHERD.)

[1:16] Ah, you are beautiful, my beloved, truly lovely. Our couch is green; [1:17] the beams of our house are cedar, our rafters are pine. [2:1] I am a rose of Sharon, a lily of the valleys.

KING SOLOMON

[2:2] As a lily among brambles, so is my love among maidens.

SHULAMMITE

[2:3] As an apple tree among the trees of the wood, so is my beloved among young men. With great delight I sat in his shadow, and his fruit was sweet to my taste. [2:4] He brought me to the banqueting house, and his intention toward me was love. [2:5] Sustain me with raisins, refresh me with apples; for I am faint with love. [2:6] O that his left hand were under my head, and that his right hand embraced me!

(KING SOLOMON gives up. The EUNUCHS return the SHULAMMITE to the HAREM.)

Act 2, Scene 2: Resist the Oppressor

SETTING: The chambers of KING SOLOMON's HAREM in his palace in Jerusalem.

AT RISE: The women of the HAREM have gathered to see what the SHULAMMITE thought of her first encounter with KING SOLOMON.

SHULAMMITE

(The SHULAMMITE addresses the HAREM.)

²:⁷ **I adjure you, O daughters of Jerusalem, by the gazelles or the wild does: do not stir up or awaken love until it is ready!**

Act 3: The Good Shepherd

Scene 1: The Shulammite Sends the Shepherd Away

SETTING: KING SOLOMON's country estate located in the Northern Kingdom in or near Lebanon. It is also near Shulem, the SHULAMMITE's hometown. The SHULAMMITE has been taken along with other members of the HAREM to the country estate in preparation for the King's arrival.

AT RISE: The SHULAMMITE is in the HAREM's bedroom when she hears the far off voice of her SHEPHERD. Other members of the HAREM are around, but they pay no attention to what the SHULAMMITE is doing. She peers out of her bedroom window into the hills. She is ecstatic that her SHEPHERD has found her.

SHULAMMITE

[2:8] The voice of my beloved! Look, he comes, leaping upon the mountains, bounding over the hills. [2:9] My beloved is like a gazelle or a young stag. Look, there he stands behind our wall, gazing in at the windows, looking through the lattice. [2:10] My beloved speaks and says to me . . .

SHEPHERD

Arise, my love, my fair one, and come away; [2:11] for now the winter is past, the rain is over and gone. [2:12] The flowers appear on the earth; the time of singing has come, and the voice of the turtledove is heard in our land. [2:13] The fig tree puts forth its figs, and the vines are in blossom; they give forth fragrance. Arise, my love, my fair one, and come away. [2:14] O my dove, in the clefts of the rock, in the covert of the cliff, let me see your face, let me hear your voice; for your voice is sweet, and your face is lovely. [2:15] Catch us the foxes, the little foxes, that ruin the vineyards—for our vineyards are in blossom.

SHULAMMITE

[2:16] My beloved is mine and I am his; he pastures his flock among the lilies. [2:17] Until the day breathes and the shadows flee, turn, my beloved, be like a gazelle or a young stag on the cleft mountains.

Act 3, Scene 2: The Shulammite Regrets Sending the Shepherd Away

SETTING: The HAREM's bedroom inside KING SOLOMON's country estate.

AT RISE: It is now nighttime. The SHULAMMITE is waking from sleep.

SHULAMMITE

[3:1] Upon my bed at night I sought him whom my soul loves; I sought him, but found him not; I called him, but he gave no answer. [3:2] "I will rise now and go about the city, in the streets and in the squares; I will seek him whom my soul loves." I sought him, but found him not. [3:3] The sentinels found me, as they went about in the city. "Have you seen him whom my soul loves?" [3:4] Scarcely had I passed them, when I found him whom my soul loves. I held him, and would not let him go until I brought him into my mother's house, and into the chamber of her that conceived me.

(Happy that she has found her SHEPHERD again, the SHULAMMITE once again turns to the HAREM and encourages the women to resist their situation.)

[3:5] I adjure you, O daughters of Jerusalem, by the gazelles or the wild does: do not stir up or awaken love until it is ready!

Act 4: Love Triangle

Scene 1: Solomon Seduces

SETTING: A balcony of KING SOLOMON's country estate.

AT RISE: The SHULAMMITE, along with a few members of the HAREM, is standing on a balcony of the estate watching KING SOLOMON and his great entourage approaching in the distance.

SHULAMMITE

[3:6] What is that coming up from the wilderness, like a column of smoke, perfumed with myrrh and frankincense, with all the fragrant powders of the merchant?

HAREM

[3:7] Look, it is the litter of Solomon! Around it are sixty mighty men of the mighty men of Israel, [3:8] all equipped with swords and expert in war, each with his sword at his thigh because of alarms by night. [3:9] King Solomon made himself a palanquin from the wood of Lebanon. [3:10] He made its posts of silver, its back of gold, its seat of purple; its interior was inlaid with love.

EUNUCHS

(The EUNUCHS call to the HAREM to join them at the entrance of the estate where they are to greet KING SOLOMON.)

Daughters of Jerusalem,[3:11] **come out. Look, O daughters of Zion, at King Solomon, at the crown with which his mother crowned him on the day of his wedding, on the day of the gladness of his heart.**

KING SOLOMON

(KING SOLOMON reaches his country estate. Upon seeing the SHULAMMITE, he goes over to talk to her, ignoring the rest of the HAREM.)

[4:1] **How beautiful you are, my love, how very beautiful! Your eyes are doves behind your veil. Your hair is like a flock of goats, moving down the slopes of Gilead.** [4:2] **Your teeth are like a flock of shorn ewes that have come up from the washing, all of which bear twins, and not one among them is bereaved.** [4:3] **Your lips are like a crimson thread, and your mouth is lovely. Your cheeks are like halves of a pomegranate behind your veil.** [4:4] **Your neck is like the tower of David, built in courses; on it hang a thousand bucklers, all of them shields of warriors.** [4:5] **Your two breasts are like two fawns, twins of a gazelle, that feed among the lilies.** [4:6] **Until the day breathes and the shadows flee, I will hasten to the mountain of myrrh and the hill of frankincense.** [4:7] **You are altogether beautiful, my love; there is no flaw in you.**

(The SHULAMMITE pays him no attention and the scene ends.)

Act 4, Scene 2: The Shepherd Romances

SETTING: The HAREM's bedroom inside KING SOLOMON's country estate.

AT RISE: The SHULAMMITE is in the HAREM's bedroom. She peers out her window and there the Shepherd is again.

SHEPHERD

[4:8] **Come with me from Lebanon, my bride; come with me from Lebanon. Depart from the peak of Amana, from the peak of Senir and**

Hermon, from the dens of lions, from the mountains of leopards. [4:9] You have ravished my heart, my sister, my bride, you have ravished my heart with a glance of your eyes, with one jewel of your necklace. [4:10] How sweet is your love, my sister, my bride! How much better is your love than wine, and the fragrance of your oils than any spice! [4:11] Your lips distill nectar, my bride; honey and milk are under your tongue; the scent of your garments is like the scent of Lebanon. [4:12] A garden locked is my sister, my bride, a garden locked, a fountain sealed. [4:13] Your channel is an orchard of pomegranates with all choicest fruits, henna with nard, [4:14] nard and saffron, calamus and cinnamon, with all trees of frankincense, myrrh and aloes, with all chief spices [4:15]—a garden fountain, a well of living water, and flowing streams from Lebanon.

SHULAMMITE

[4:16] Awake, O north wind, and come, O south wind! Blow upon my garden that its fragrance may be wafted abroad. Let my beloved come to his garden, and eat its choicest fruits.

SHEPHERD

[5:1] I come to my garden, my sister, my bride; I gather my myrrh with my spice, I eat my honeycomb with my honey, I drink my wine with my milk.

HAREM

Eat, friends, drink, and be drunk with love.

Act 5: The Shulammite's Nightmare

Scene 1: Beaten and Wounded

SETTING: The HAREM's bedroom inside KING SOLOMON's country estate.

AT RISE: It is nighttime. The SHULAMMITE is returning to her room. It is obvious that she has been outside. She is bruised and dirty. Her coat is missing. She wakes the HAREM to tell them what has happened.

SHULAMMITE

5:2 **I slept, but my heart was awake.**

(The SHULAMMITE reenacts what has happened for the HAREM. She listens as if she can hear knocking.)

Listen! My beloved is knocking.

SHEPHERD

"Open to me, my sister, my love, my dove, my perfect one; for my head is wet with dew, my locks with the drops of the night."

SHULAMMITE

(To the HAREM.)

5:3 **I had put off my garment; how could I put it on again? I had bathed my feet; how could I soil them?**

(The SHEPHERD reaches through the garden gate for the SHULAMMITE, begging her to open it.)

5:4 **My beloved thrust his hand into the opening, and my inmost being yearned for him.**

(The SHEPHERD withdraws his hand and disappears. The SHULAMMITE runs over to the garden gate and tries to unbolt the door, but her hands are slippery with the fancy cosmetics that she had put on her hands.)

5:5 **I arose to open to my beloved, and my hands dripped with myrrh, my fingers with liquid myrrh, upon the handles of the bolt.**

(She finally gets the gate open.)

5:6 **I opened to my beloved, but my beloved had turned and was gone.**

(She turns back to the HAREM again trying to justify herself.)

My soul failed me when he spoke. I sought him, but did not find him; I called him, but he gave no answer. 5:7 **Making their rounds in the**

city the sentinels found me; they beat me, they wounded me, they took away my mantle, those sentinels of the walls.

(Turning to the HAREM.)

5:8 I adjure you, O daughters of Jerusalem, if you find my beloved, tell him this: I am faint with love.

Act 5, Scene 2: Ridiculed

SETTING: Halls of the country estate.

AT RISE: The SHULAMMITE has been summoned to KING SOLOMON's bedroom in the country estate. She does not want to go.

HAREM

(As the SHULAMMITE is walking to his bedroom, some of the women in the HAREM follow her—taunting her.)

5:9 What is your beloved more than another beloved, O fairest among women? What is your beloved more than another beloved, that you thus adjure us?

SHULAMMITE

5:10 My beloved is all radiant and ruddy, distinguished among ten thousand. 5:11 His head is the finest gold; his locks are wavy, black as a raven. 5:12 His eyes are like doves beside springs of water, bathed in milk, fitly set. 5:13 His cheeks are like beds of spices, yielding fragrance. His lips are lilies, distilling liquid myrrh. 5:14 His arms are rounded gold, set with jewels. His body is ivory work, encrusted with sapphires. 5:15 His legs are alabaster columns, set upon bases of gold. His appearance is like Lebanon, choice as the cedars. 5:16 His speech is most sweet, and he is altogether desirable. This is my beloved and this is my friend, O daughters of Jerusalem.

HAREM

(The HAREM continues to mock the SHULAMMITE.)

⁶:¹ **Where has your beloved gone, O fairest among women? Which way has your beloved turned, that we may seek him with you?**

SHULAMMITE

⁶:² **My beloved has gone down to his garden, to the beds of spices, to pasture his flock in the gardens, and to gather lilies. ⁶:³ I am my beloved's and my beloved is mine; he pastures his flock among the lilies.**

(She reaches SOLOMON's bedroom. He is waiting for her. The HAREM watches on from outside curious what will happen when she rejects him. No one has ever rejected the King before.)

KING SOLOMON

(He wants to try and convince her one more time, but her constant rejection has started to frustrate him. He doesn't know how to deal with it any longer.)

⁶:⁴ **You are beautiful as Tirzah, my love, comely as Jerusalem, terrible as an army with banners. ⁶:⁵ Turn away your eyes from me, for they overwhelm me! Your hair is like a flock of goats, moving down the slopes of Gilead. ⁶:⁶ Your teeth are like a flock of ewes, that have come up from the washing; all of them bear twins, and not one among them is bereaved. ⁶:⁷ Your cheeks are like halves of a pomegranate behind your veil. ⁶:⁸ There are sixty queens and eighty concubines, and maidens without number. ⁶:⁹ My dove, my perfect one, is the only one, the darling of her mother, flawless to her that bore her. The maidens saw her and called her happy; the queens and concubines also, and they praised her.**

HAREM

(The HAREM sarcastically answers KING SOLOMON. They do not share his admiration of the SHULAMMITE.)

⁶:¹⁰ **"Who is this that looks forth like the dawn, fair as the moon, bright as the sun, terrible as an army with banners?"**

Act 5, Scene 3: Enslaved by Desire

SETTING: In KING SOLOMON's bedroom, the SHULAMMITE remembers a nut orchard in her hometown north of Jerusalem. This flashback takes place prior to the beginning of the Song.

AT RISE: The SHULAMMITE retells the story of being captured by KING SOLOMON's men.

SHULAMMITE

[6:11] I went down to the nut orchard, to look at the blossoms of the valley, to see whether the vines had budded, whether the pomegranates were in bloom. [6:12] Before I was aware, my fancy set me in a chariot beside my prince.

Act 6: Love Wins

Scene 1: Rejecting the Oppressor

SETTING: The entrance to KING SOLOMON's country estate.

AT RISE: The VILLAGERS from the SHULAMMITE's hometown of Shulem have heard that the SHULAMMITE is at KING SOLOMON's estate. They have gathered at the entrance to see her.

VILLAGERS

(The VILLAGERS form a chorus calling her to come to where they can see her.)

[6:13] Return, return, O Shulammite! Return, return, that we may look upon you.

SHULAMMITE

(She hears the VILLAGERS from a balcony of the palace and cries to them.)

Why should you look upon the Shulammite?

VILLAGERS

As upon a dance before two armies. [7:1] How graceful are your feet in sandals, O queenly maiden! Your rounded thighs are like jewels, the work of a master hand. [7:2] Your navel is a rounded bowl that never lacks mixed wine. Your belly is a heap of wheat, encircled with lilies. [7:3] Your two breasts are like two fawns, twins of a gazelle. [7:4] Your neck is like an ivory tower. Your eyes are pools in Heshbon, by the gate of Bath-rabbim. Your nose is like a tower of Lebanon, overlooking Damascus. [7:5] Your head crowns you like Carmel, and your flowing locks are like purple; a king is held captive in the tresses.

KING SOLOMON

(KING SOLOMON appears and makes one last appeal to the SHULAMMITE.)

[7:6] How fair and pleasant you are, O loved one, delectable maiden! [7:7] You are stately as a palm tree, and your breasts are like its clusters. [7:8] I say I will climb the palm tree and lay hold of its branches. Oh, may your breasts be like clusters of the vine, and the scent of your breath like apples, [7:9] and your kisses like the best wine that goes down smoothly, gliding over lips and teeth.

SHULAMMITE

(Rejects KING SOLOMON.)

[7:10] I am my beloved's, and his desire is for me.

Act 6, Scene 2: Commitment to the Shepherd

SETTING: The road into the SHULAMMITE's hometown.

AT RISE: The SHULAMMITE has been set free. She is leaving KING SOLOMON's country estate and walking to her village. She calls to her SHEPHERD who she can see coming for her. The HAREM is standing with her.

SHULAMMITE

(SHULAMMITE calls to the SHEPHERD.)

7:11 Come, my beloved, let us go forth into the fields, and lodge in the villages; 7:12 let us go out early to the vineyards, and see whether the vines have budded, whether the grape blossoms have opened and the pomegranates are in bloom. There I will give you my love. 7:13 The mandrakes give forth fragrance, and over our doors are all choice fruits, new as well as old, which I have laid up for you, O my beloved. 8:1 O that you were like a brother to me, who nursed at my mother's breast! If I met you outside, I would kiss you, and no one would despise me. 8:2 I would lead you and bring you into the house of my mother, and into the chamber of the one who bore me. I would give you spiced wine to drink, the juice of my pomegranates. 8:3 O that his left hand were under my head, and that his right hand embraced me!

(The SHULAMMITE warns the HAREM one last time.)

8:4 I adjure you, O daughters of Jerusalem, do not stir up or awaken love until it is ready!

(The SHULAMMITE leans on her SHEPHERD as they walk to their village.)

VILLAGERS

8:5 Who is that coming up from the wilderness, leaning upon her beloved?

SHULAMMITE

(Speaking to her SHEPHERD.)

Under the apple tree, I awakened you. There your mother was in labor with you; there she who bore you was in labor. 8:6 Set me as a seal upon your heart, as a seal upon your arm; for love is strong as death, passion fierce as the grave. Its flashes are flashes of fire, a raging flame. 8:7 Many waters cannot quench love, neither can floods drown it. If one offered for love all the wealth of his house, it would be utterly scorned.

VILLAGERS

(The VILLLAGERS meet the SHULAMMITE bringing with them a young GIRL, who may someday face a similar ordeal. They ask the SHULAMMITE for wisdom.)

[8:8] We have a little sister, and she has no breasts. What shall we do for our sister, on the day when she is spoken for? [8:9] If she is a wall, we will build upon her a battlement of silver; but if she is a door, we will enclose her with boards of cedar.

SHULAMMITE

(Speaking to the GIRL.)

[8:10] I was a wall, and my breasts were like towers; then I was in his eyes as one who brings peace. [8:11] Solomon had a vineyard at Baal-hamon; he entrusted the vineyard to keepers; each one was to bring for its fruit a thousand pieces of silver. [8:12] My vineyard, my very own, is for myself; you, O Solomon, may have the thousand, and the keepers of the fruit two hundred!

SHEPHERD

[8:13] O you who dwell in the gardens, my companions are listening for your voice; let me hear it.

SHULAMMITE

[8:14] Make haste, my beloved, and be like a gazelle or a young stag upon the mountains of spices!

Lectio Divina

Caleb's father, the pastor in the African-American community where Caleb had grown up, embraced an interpretation of the Song of Solomon that turned out to be especially informative in helping his community overcome the effects of injustices against African-Americans. Traditional interpretations of the Song of Solomon glorified the slave master and did nothing to dismantle oppression. By holding onto these traditional inter-pretations, we may learn harmful and erroneous lessons about God and ourselves. Letting God speak to us through Scripture is essential to learning correct lessons from Scripture. Lectio Divina is a great tool for giving the Holy Spirit a time and place to make Scripture come alive for us and lead us to the truth.

How to Practice Lectio Divina

Lectio Divina has four steps:

1. Ask God for wisdom.

2. Slowly read the Scripture for the day (see Days 1–5 below for details) aloud several times listening for God to speak to you through it. Usu-ally two or three times are enough. Allow a word, phrase, or idea to come into your thoughts. Jot down what comes to mind in your jour-nal. Note: Use the version of the Song of Solomon printed in chapter 4 so that you are reading it as Caleb understood it.

43

3. Ask God to show you why this word, phrase, or idea is in your thoughts. Let it interact with your memories and experiences. Do not be afraid of what may seem at first to be a distraction. Explore how it all relates. Give all thoughts to God and listen for God to show you what is being revealed to you. Journal.

4. Read what you have journaled back to God and ask God for power to apply what you have learned to your life. Journal about how God is empowering you to apply this to your life.

Days 1–5

There are eight chapters in the Song of Solomon. Take two chapters a day practicing Lectio Divina using those chapters. On day 5, read the entire book practicing Lectio Divina.

ACT 1

The Palace In Jerusalem

What do you think? If a shepherd has a hundred sheep, and one of them has gone astray, does he not leave the ninety-nine on the mountains and go in search of the one that went astray? And if he finds it, truly I tell you, he rejoices over it more than over the ninety-nine that never went astray. So it is not the will of your Father in heaven that one of these little ones should be lost.

—Matthew 18:12 –14

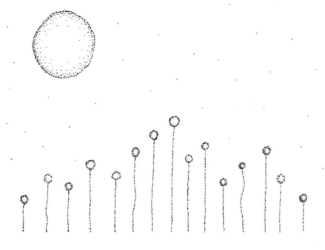

5

The Harem

Song 1:2–8

SETTING: The chambers of KING SOLOMON's HAREM within his palace in Jerusalem.[1]

AT RISE: KING SOLOMON enters the chambers of the HAREM to pick out his lover for the day.

HAREM

(The concubines of the HAREM long to be chosen by KING SOLOMON.[2] Upon seeing KING SOLOMON, the HAREM whispers to one another excitedly.)

---

1. Fletcher, *Women in the Bible,* under entry: "King Solomon's Palace in Jerusalem." Fletcher writes that King Solomon's palace was more extravagant and took longer to construct than the temple, which he built in Jerusalem. His wives and concubines were housed together in the palace, but separated from King Solomon. Both the palace and temple were built in a large enclosed area to the north of Jerusalem called the Temple Mount.

2. Ibid., under entry: "King Solomon's Harem." Harem life was a purposeless life in which the women waited around with hundreds of other women hoping that the king would take notice of them. Their status in the harem depended on the king's favor. They were anxious to spend time with the king in hopes that they might elevate their status, conceive a child, be rewarded with jewels and other gifts, or be asked to travel with him. A child to raise would give the woman meaningful purpose. In addition, even something that resembled love—sex for just an occasional night—was better than no affection at all. Therefore when the king came looking for a partner, the women wanted to impress him.

1:2 Let him kiss me with the kisses of his mouth!

(To get KING SOLOMON to notice them, they begin calling out to him.)

For your love is better than wine, 1:3 your anointing oils are fragrant, your name is perfume poured out;

EUNUCHS

(The EUNUCHS flatter KING SOLOMON.)[3]

Therefore, the maidens love you.[4]

SHULAMMITE

(The SHULAMMITE is new in the HAREM. She huddles in the corner alone. She doesn't want to be KING SOLOMON's lover. We hear her desperately cry out to her absent SHEPHERD to rescue her.)

1:4 Draw me after you, let us make haste. The king has brought me into his chambers.

HAREM

(The HAREM ignores her cries and calls to KING SOLOMON again.)

We will exult and rejoice in you; we will extol your love more than wine;

EUNUCHS

(The EUNUCHS flatter the King again.)

Rightly do they love you.

3. It was important for the eunuchs to stay in King Solomon's good graces by ensuring that the concubines under their charge were desirable to the King. Therefore, for good measure, the eunuchs pour out lots of flattery upon the King.

4. "Therefore the maidens love you" can also be translated "No wonder the maidens love you" as is done in the NIV translation.

(KING SOLOMON picks the SHULAMMITE to be his lover for the day and leaves the chamber alone. The EUNUCHS stay to ensure that the SHULAMMITE will be presentable for KING SOLOMON.)[5]

SHULAMMITE

(The SHULAMMITE begins to change to go meet with KING SOLOMON for the first time. The SHULAMMITE responds to the way the HAREM looks at her.)[6]

1:5 I am black and beautiful, O daughters of Jerusalem, like the tents of Kedar, like the curtains of Solomon.[7] 1:6 Do not gaze at me because I am dark, because the sun has gazed on me. My mother's sons were angry with me; they made me keeper of the vineyards, but my own vineyard I have not kept![8]

(Turning from the HAREM, she cries for her absent SHEPHERD again.)

1:7 Tell me, you whom my soul loves, where you pasture your flock, where you make it lie down at noon; for why should I be like one who is veiled beside the flocks of your companions?[9]

5. King Solomon, seeing his newest concubine huddled in the corner crying out to her Beloved, is delighted that he has a challenge before him. For King Solomon, the chase is what turns him on. He could rape her, but he won't. That would make an enemy out of her. It feeds his ego to lure her into begging for him like the other concubines.

6. The Shulammite knows that the women in the Harem are both jealous that she has been chosen and disgusted with her rustic peasant appearance. She is not covered in makeup as they are. Nor does she wear the latest fashion or expensive jewelry. Worst of all, her skin is unfashionably black.

7. Ginsburg, *The Song of Songs*, 133. The Shulammite compares her skin to the tents of Kedar. In 1857, Ginsburg wrote that the tents of Kedar were "to this day" made from shaggy black goat hair.

8. The Shulammite has not had a glamorous life prior to her capture. Her own brothers have mistreated her making her work so hard in the fields that she had no time to take care of herself. However, back home, she had a family, a village, and her beloved Shepherd.

9. Pope, *Song of Songs* 330–31. "One who is veiled" can be interpreted as "a prostitute." The Shulammite is desperate. If her Shepherd does not come for her, if she cannot escape and find him, she will be forced to consummate her relationship to the King as his concubine. In her assessment, this means that she will have taken on the status equal to "one who is veiled"—a prostitute. If this happens, she feels that she will no longer be acceptable to her Shepherd. She will be an outcast only fit to live beside the flocks of the Shepherd's companions, never in the tent of the Shepherd. She is desperate to find a way out of the situation.

HAREM

(The HAREM sarcastically tells her how to find her SHEPHERD.)[10]

[1:8] If you do not know, O fairest among women, follow the tracks of the flock, and pasture your kids beside the shepherds' tents.

✱✱✱

Although Congressman Morgan's office was about an hour walk from my English basement apartment, I looked forward to walking it. No matter how long I lived in DC, I never lost the feelings of wonder generated by this extraordinary city with its marble, granite, and sandstone buildings. I headed south until I came upon Virginia Avenue and followed it until I reached the National Mall. It was an iconic stroll passing by the Washington Monument, the Smithsonian Museums, the National Museum of Art, the United States Capitol, and the Supreme Court buildings. As I passed each government building, I imagined what important affairs of state might be on the docket for the next week. The museums, which I had visited countless times, caused me to recall the world-class collections of art and historic relics they housed. There was nothing else like Washington, DC in the entire world.

All too soon, I reached the Cannon House Office Building. My credentials got me through a rather upbeat security guard's inspection and directions to Congressman Morgan's outer office. The guard's directions sent me the scenic route through the rotunda flooded with light from the oculus several stories above and then up one of the twin marble staircases and down the hall to one of fourteen three-room suites granted to the most honorable and longstanding members of the house.

It was Sunday afternoon and the building was mostly empty except for a few staffers here and there. Congressman Morgan's assistant, who had been with him in the airport, was seated in blue jeans and a sports coat at the suite's reception desk. His feet were propped up on the desk and he was reading the Washington Post.

Oddly, for me at least, I had arrived twenty minutes early and stood quietly in the doorway for several seconds before he realized I was there.

---

10. The harem does not understand why the Shulammite wants to go back to her lowly Shepherd when she could be with the glamorous King. They suspect that she thinks that she is too good to be part of the harem.

For once, I was not worried about being bored. In fact, I had hoped for some time alone to savor this remarkable opportunity before me. When he saw me, he jumped up, embarrassed not to have known that he was being watched, shook my hand, and offered me coffee. Carrying my own, I answered by smiling and lifting my thermos to show him.

He introduced himself as Reggie and told me Congressman Morgan was on the phone, but would be available soon. He was much more relaxed and jovial than he had been at the airport and every bit as good looking. I liked him. He was a serious but happy person. It was only a minute or two before Congressman Morgan beckoned us to his office. From the tone of his voice, I could tell he was excited about this little project.

"Come on in!" He stood from behind his desk and shook my hand. Behind him, there hung five black and white photographs each in an identical frame. The photographs had been taken at different times, but each showed Congressman Morgan with a different dignitary. I counted two Presidents, a Secretary of State, a Prime Minister of Israel, and a Chancellor of Germany. He caught me looking at the photographs.

"Impressive aren't they?"

"Yes!" I couldn't hide how impressed I was so I deflected my admiration by making a joke, "And I bet at night when you go home they come to life and have important discussions on world matters."

"Indeed they must!" he laughed. "So young lady, are you going to write my story?"

I smiled uncontrollably from ear to ear, "You knew I would, Congressman Morgan."

"Sit down then. But from here on out, you call me Caleb."

"Done."

In the airport, I had let Caleb talk without interrupting him. I had had no choice; he had talked in a steady stream of consciousness without coming up for air except for short lunch and bathroom breaks. I hadn't had a tape recorder and had taken very few notes merely because he talked too fast. However, I knew that if I were going to write his story, I would have to get him to start over and tape it this time. I asked him if that would be okay. He said yes. We also agreed to meet every Sunday morning for two hours from here on out.

Caleb wanted to talk about compensation, but I refused saying that since this was my first endeavor at anything like this, he should wait until he saw what I produced. He motioned to Reggie to get something in the outer office. It was a simple one-page contract—more like a friendly agreement. We would agree that as long as he was alive, I wouldn't publish anything about the Congressman without his approval, but that whatever compensation the project generated would belong to me. I expressed again that I wasn't interested in compensation and he expressed that neither was he. He suggested that I could always give any profits away to my favorite charity. He wouldn't have it any other way. He signed the agreement and handed it to me. I signed too.

Then we began. I explained that I had done some research in the theology stacks at Georgetown learning a bit about the Shulammite and the Song of Solomon. I had to confess that though I grew up in Sunday school and youth group, never once did I ever read or hear anyone teach about the Song of Solomon.

"That's because people don't understand it!" replied Caleb. "They don't know its life transforming capabilities."

Part of me wondered if he was taking this whole thing too far and another part of me found him completely grounded. "If I had to summarize what I have already gathered from our conversation at the airport, I would say that you believe that by weaving your story with the Song of Solomon, it can help people see a need for a deeper connection with their Creator."

"I do. This is jumping the gun a bit, but stick with me. If a deeper relationship with God is all one takes away from the Song that is outstanding. However, you will see that there is *even more* to be learned through the Song."

"Can you summarize what else is to be learned through the Song?"

"Well, without even being aware of the trap, most Christians participate in what I call 'unjust systems.' Either intentionally or unintentionally, they become entrapped in them. These systems are against the good that God desires for humankind. I believe that God sent Jesus to rescue us from unjust systems so that our lives can reflect the Kingdom of God. For instance, in the Lord's Prayer, Jesus taught his disciples to pray, 'Thy kingdom come, thy will be done on earth as it is in heaven.' My dad taught that this meant that we should be living out the Kingdom of God in the here and now. My hope is that my story will challenge those who read it to choose the Kingdom of God over the unjust systems that rule this earth."

"How do we recognize one of these unjust systems?" I tried to hide my hesitation to buy into what seemed to me to be a mythological cosmic battle between good and evil: the Kingdom of God vs Unjust World Systems. Either I hid my hesitation well, or he was expecting it. He didn't flinch.

"Unjust systems are powered by selfish lust and one is seduced into taking part in them. Within them, one must earn acceptance and love—at least what passes for love (love isn't truly love if you have to earn it). Anyway, if one lives under an unjust system for too long, that person can become so broken that they become unable to even see themselves or others as deserving love or justice."

My eyes must have grown wider as he talked. It seemed—well, I don't know exactly what it seemed. It seemed over-the-top, down-to-earth, holy, and crazy all at once.

Reggie was watching me. If Caleb hadn't caught my wavering, Reggie did. It prompted Reggie to jump in when Caleb stopped to take a sip of his coffee. "In an unjust system there are orchestrated winners and losers. The losers will not have their needs met while the winners will have more than enough. On the other hand, systems that are part of the Kingdom of God—or as I like to say, 'Reign of God'[11]—will demonstrate the unconditional love of the Creator to everyone who participates in them. The concerns of everyone will be met and no one will benefit on the backs of others. Most importantly, a place in the Kingdom of God is not earned, but a result of God's grace."

"Can you define what the Kingdom of God is?"

"Well, first of all, the reason I prefer the term Reign of God is that the Kingdom of God is not a place—it is what happens within us when we let God reign and what works itself out of us through what we do and how we act. Once Jesus was asked by the Pharisees when the Kingdom of God was coming, and he answered, 'The Kingdom of God is not coming with things that can be observed; nor will they say, "Look, here it is!" or "There it is!" For, in fact, the Kingdom of God is among you.'[12] The Kingdom of God isn't a term that is used in the Song, but it describes the spiritual place where the

---

11. The Greek word, *basileia*, translated in the New Testament as *kingdom* might be better translated as *reign*. Kingdom brings to mind a geographically located place, whereas reign better captures a spiritual way of allowing God to reign within us.

12. Luke 17:20–21.

Shepherd is inviting the Shulammite. When the Shulammite says 'yes' to the Shepherd's love for her, it creates in her what two thousand years later Jesus coins the Reign of God. It is what our lives are transformed into when we, like the Shulammite, say 'yes' to the Good Shepherd. It is a spiritual space where we can become our best selves."

Reggie stopped, but I knew he had more to say. I made eye contact and with wide eyes and a slight movement of my head, I encouraged him to continue.

"I am not sure the rest of what I have to say is worth saying. Nonetheless, I have been developing a theory that I can't yet prove wrong. It seems to me that unjust systems are generally complex, grand, gaudy, and filled with chaos and intrigue. King Solomon and his harem were like this. The Shepherd and the Shulammite were not—they were simple, straightforward, humble, gentle, and uncomplicated. In addition, the unjust system manipulates, whereas the Reign of God is always forthright."

"Reggie, I would agree with you," nodded Caleb. "Unjust systems require that you know your way through the land mines—the culture, the rituals, and the subtext. To be successful in them you must dress the part, speak the language, network successfully, and know who to kowtow to. The Kingdom of God is different. You can be yourself without fear of reprisal."

I took a breath, looked back and forth at both of the men, and was hooked once again. They were not only telling me something very important to them, but they both believed what they were saying. I didn't understand it all yet, but what I did know deep inside of myself was that I was going to walk away from this experience with wisdom that would serve me the rest of my life.

Caleb picked up where he had left off, "Shortly after I confiscated the amphetamines in the locker room, I headed to the front office to turn the drugs over to the athletic director."

★★★

Remembering halfway there that the athletic director was away from the school that morning, Caleb decided to take the drugs to the principal instead. However, as Caleb passed by the athletic director's office, the door was open. Caleb could see that he had just arrived and was reaching for a ringing phone. Caleb stuck his head in and with a big smile, the athletic director motioned for Caleb to have a seat. Caleb glanced around the office while the phone call finished up. The office was sterile with a single photograph sitting on the desk. The photograph was of an attractive, heavyset woman holding an equally husky toddler.

The athletic director put his hand over the phone, leaned forward toward Caleb, and whispered, "It's Rufus Bennett with a ten-thousand dollar donation to upgrade the stadium parking lot." The athletic director shrugged his shoulders and added, "I didn't even know it needed upgrading," then put his focus back on the phone conversation.

Caleb was becoming suspicious of the name Bennett. Not only was it the name of the ace selling the steroids, but there had also been a Hallie Bennett on the search committee who had hired Caleb. Georgia was a state that put a high value on athletics. Coaches weren't hired like other teachers. A committee was formed from a pool of community movers and shakers. Their job was to search out the best coaches they could find and interview them.

Hallie Bennett had been the head of his search committee. She was an eye-catching bleached-blonde in her early forties, who was street smart, but not particularly book smart. She was unconcerned that others might think her pushy. She used tough, often vulgar words in everyday conversations. Caleb had even observed her during the interview process speaking down to others on the committee. It was obvious that she felt privileged and believed that she had nothing to gain by using a bit of decorum and patience with others.

When the phone call ended, the athletic director asked Caleb if he had met Rufus yet—as if everyone should know Rufus. Leaning back in his chair, the athletic director confirmed that Hallie was Rufus's daughter-in-law. He alluded to something else about Hallie. Hallie liked playing the field and everyone knew it—except maybe Jake, her husband. Caleb didn't react to the gossip and instead took on a serious tone as he began to describe his morning.

As if on cue, the school maintenance man happened by. He was the first black man Caleb had seen at Grandville High. The athletic director motioned for him to come in and hear the story. The maintenance man identified the Bennett in the locker room as Rufus's grandson. He was also Hallie's son. But having Rufus as a grandfather was obviously more important to the school's maintenance man than having Hallie as a mom. No one mentioned that Jake was the boy's father. It was obvious that Jake wasn't important in the equation.

To Caleb's surprise, neither the athletic director nor the maintenance man flinched as he told them about the drug transaction in the locker room. Indifference was the only way Caleb could describe it. The maintenance man said nothing on the subject, got up, and laid the stub of a student parking ticket on the athletic director's desk. He congratulated Caleb for landing "the best athletic program" in the state, then left slowly meandering down the hall looking as if life depressed him.

"Look Caleb, Rufus runs this town and this school. He knows about his grandson's use of amphetamines. Heck, he probably gets the drugs for him. I wouldn't want my kid taking them. But believe me—Rufus is going to take care of you."

"You are aware that amphetamines will hurt those boys? More than one athlete has died from them. Over time, they cause paranoia, aggression, hallucinations—even dental problems. Oh and by the way, they *are* illegal." Caleb struggled to control his feelings of contempt for a school administration that would look the other way while a boy was being drugged by his grandfather.

The athletic director, to emphasize what he was about to say, walked around his desk and put his hand on Caleb's shoulder, "Caleb, just let it go. The Bennetts' disregard for the law has been going on for years, if not generations. Jake and Rufus both played sports at this very high school. You can't stop them. They know what they are doing."

Then immediately in a brighter tone while holding out his hand to Caleb, "Mr. Morgan, I hope you know that you really have landed the best job in the state! You have no idea how much you are going to love it here. Rufus handpicked you. You are all set up for great perks. Enjoy it!" Caleb shook his hand, but not convincingly.

Caleb walked back to his office outside the locker rooms. Could it be true that this city, the school administrators, and now he were all being held captive by the will of someone named "Rufus"? Who was this guy? The day had gone from sunny and fresh to dark and gloomy. He felt overwhelmed to say the least. He sat down in his office. One wall was glass with glass shelves that looked into the hall. On the glass shelves were various awards, pictures, and trophies. He reentered the hall to look them over. In one of the pictures, he located Rufus Bennett. He had made All-State back in the Dark Ages. There was an award given to Jake Bennett sitting on the shelf above Rufus—a "Distinguished Alumni Award." It didn't say what Jake had done to distinguish himself, but it had been bestowed upon him in the past year.

Caleb did the only thing he knew to do. He closed his door, turned his chair around so his back was facing the glass shelves that separated his office from the hall, and prayed. He didn't know exactly what to pray for. Deliverance from this new job? Forgiveness for being seduced to a higher paying job? For the boys who were taking amphetamines? For the administration who were held captive by Rufus's influence? For Rufus? Not knowing what to say to God, he simply told God what was going on, asked God to be near, and left it at that.

As he finished praying, his mind flashed back to his days as a starting quarterback at Harrelson High in Colquitt County, Georgia. It was a poor county and an even poorer all black public high school. His love had never truly been baseball, but back then, if you were an athlete at a small high school, you could try your hand at every sport. So he had played his fair share—in fact, he played every year in high school along with football. But football was what he had excelled at.

One thing was for certain, Caleb's dad would never have approved of anyone taking illegal drugs. Doc was strict. In Caleb's high school years, he could not even get Doc to approve of the innocent beer parties that went on out at Indian Lake. In fact, when Doc caught Caleb meeting the older boys on the football team out there for a beer, Caleb was forced to tell his mother what he had done and promise that he wouldn't go out drinking any more. The hurt and worried look on her face was all he needed to keep his promise to her. These memories stirred in Caleb the desire to do something to help these boys at Grandville. Therefore, the next morning he headed directly to the principal's office—this time bypassing his boss.

Upon arriving at the principal's suite, Caleb found that her secretary was away from the reception desk. However, Caleb could hear voices coming from the principal's office. He realized that the secretary, athletic director, and principal were all inside talking about him.

"He is going to be a problem," said the principal.

The secretary responded, "Why did they hire a black man from a black high school for this job anyway? Doesn't that make us white trash?"

The principal added, "Seriously. Why did Rufus Bennett want a black man coaching at Grandville?"

The athletic director, trying to move things along, said, "It's a whole new ballgame girls! But Rufus picked him, Rufus likes him, and that is going to have to be good enough for all of us. Let's get back to work."

Caleb was standing in the doorway as the athletic director and secretary turned to leave. Upon seeing him, they stopped in their tracks. They had to. Caleb was blocking their exit. The secretary cackled nervously and looked at Caleb's feet. The principal and head coach looked at each other in silence. The tension could be cut with a knife.

Caleb spoke. "I guess that I don't have to tell you that I'm having a really lousy first week: boys doing drugs in the locker room and racist comments in the principal's office. I never thought I'd say this, but I'm sorta missing my old job where I was underpaid and my athletic program was underfunded. But where I come from I was at least respected." All six-foot-four-inches of his large muscular frame filled the doorway. There was silence, but just for thirty seconds.

Then the principal spoke, "If we aren't good enough for you Caleb, maybe your old job is still open."

"Maybe it is."

Breaking the tension, a voice from behind him spoke. "Welcome Coach Morgan!" The voice was loud and friendly—unaware of what had just transpired. "My name is Jake Bennett. You know my wife, Hallie." Caleb turned to see Hallie and Jake. Jake was offering his hand to Caleb. Jake had an interesting face—ruggedly handsome, but unpleasant looking too—a meanness shimmering just under the surface. His eyes wanted to sparkle, which told Caleb that being mean wasn't in his nature. But since they didn't sparkle, Caleb guessed there had been many dreadfully unhappy years behind Jake.

Caleb offered his hand in return, "Great to meet you Jake." Then looking at Hallie, who winked at him, added, "Hallie, I trust you're well."

Hallie answered, "I'm damn fine now that you're here." She hugged him. That was a bold move. White women didn't hug black men. Not ever. The hug was longer and tighter than she should have hugged him. She wanted the fact that she had headed up the committee that hired a black man to be in the face of everyone else. "I have business to take care of so I will leave you and Jake alone to get to know each other."

At first glance, Hallie seemed like the ultimate humanitarian—a non-racist among racists. She seemed bold and determined to champion the Negro cause. But as Caleb would soon find out Hallie just liked to shock people. She was no more a humanitarian than anyone else in Grandville. She just liked the attention of being bold and improper. There was nothing noble about her.

Caleb, still blocking the exit from the principal's office, looked back at the threesome standing behind him. The look on his face made it obvious that he was not done with them, but that he wanted to talk to Jake. "Jake, how about we take a walk back to my office?" Then looking back at the group again while speaking to Jake, he added, "Something happened that I think you should know about."

Arriving at his office, Caleb told Jake about the amphetamine transaction. He made sure that Jake understood that his son was not just a user, but a trafficker too. He made certain Jake was aware of the health risks and the law. It wasn't clear whether Jake was going to be mad at Caleb or not—until Caleb was done. What looked like meanness on Jake's face slowly slid off.

"Caleb, you don't know this city or my family." Jake looked down at his knees and shook his head.

"Why don't you tell me about it?"

Jake wavered. It seemed he wasn't sure if he should open up to Caleb or not. Perhaps it was because Caleb had told him the truth about the drugs. Perhaps it was because he hadn't had anyone else to talk to in a long time. Or maybe it was because Caleb was a black guy that no one in town was going to trust or believe so telling him just didn't matter. Whatever it was, in that split second, Jake decided to tell Caleb.

Jake talked for the next thirty minutes. He explained that Rufus, whom he called "Daddy," had moved to Carroll County as a child. "Daddy" was said with a deep southern drawl. It was a typical name for one's father in the south—if you were white. It had never stopped sounding absurd to Caleb when coming out of the mouth of a grown man. It just went along with everything else Caleb was learning about Rufus and his kowtowing minions.

Rufus had moved to Carroll County his junior year of high school, played sports there, and made the 1912 All-State football team. He was on the path to greatness. He even had a full scholarship to play at Georgia Tech. Then he was injured in an automobile accident. Rufus had been driving. Drunk. His high school sweetheart had been in his brand new convertible with him. She was thrown from the car and died instantly. Rufus lived, obviously, but lost a leg. His dreams of going anywhere in the sports world were over.

"People who know him well—like my grandma, his own mom—say Daddy was different after that. Ruthless and selfish. But you wouldn't know it to talk to him. Not unless he has a problem with you. He acts gracious, generous, and even self-deprecating to those who don't get in his way." Jake stopped and seemed to be thinking about what he had just said.

Then he went on, "Anyway, Daddy finished the engineering program at Tech and came back home to build a highly successful regional business here. He helps a lot of people. But he demands your soul in return."

To keep the conversation going, Caleb motioned to the award in Jake's honor sitting on the glass shelf, "Looks like you played baseball here too."

"That I did. But I didn't do real well. Daddy wanted me to fill his footsteps. His game had been football, but I liked baseball more. He didn't care which sport I played as long as I was a rising star. But, in the long run, I just didn't have what it took. No one had ever heard of amphetamines back in the late thirties. But I probably would have taken them too. Daddy would have gotten them for me just like he gets them for my son. I lifted weights and worked out incessantly. But I didn't have the raw genetic material that Daddy had had."

Jake was ashamed that he hadn't fulfilled his father's dreams. Then he added, "Caleb, maybe you can change things here. Talk some sense into people. God knows we need it."

Just then, Hallie walked in looking for Jake. Her presence ended any more heart-to-heart conversation between the men. Sitting down next to Jake, her short skirt slid up her leg exposing a toned, but large thigh. She glanced at her leg and then up at Caleb raising her eyebrow when she caught him unwillingly looking in her direction.

"Hallie flirts with everyone, Caleb. Don't take offense."

"I have a reputation," smiled Hallie cattily.

Jake, looking at Hallie, smiled uncomfortably, shook his head, and then looked at Caleb knowingly. "Like I said, you don't know my family or this town."

Hallie stood, obviously disgusted with whatever it was Jake had been telling Caleb, and told Jake to meet her in the parking lot in three minutes. She needed to run one last errand in the school building. Looking back she quipped, "Don't let Jake fool you. He loves my wild side. Without me he is stuck in this boring town with these boring people—most of whom he is related to."

"That is another sad truth," mumbled Jake as he got up to follow her.

***

I asked Caleb if we could pause his story while I asked him a few questions. He agreed. I wanted him, in his own words, to begin connecting his story with the Shulammite's story. He said okay, but first he wanted to know what I found significant about the Shulammite so far. Since he had wanted a female's perspective, I gave him my first impression from that angle.

"Well, I was taken aback that this peasant girl knows she is beautiful."

"Yes! Here she is a newly captured slave, enslaved among the most beautiful women King Solomon could find. She knows they are looking down their noses at her, yet she stands up to them and says, 'I am black and beautiful.'"[13]

"I think this is key to being able to overcome one's circumstances—to know that you are beautiful—and I am not talking looks here. Somehow this young peasant woman has confidence in herself—knows who she is despite being poor and despite having had no time to care for herself."

A pleased smile spread over Caleb's face and his eyes danced, "How do you suppose she knew that she was beautiful? What if we could instill that knowledge in every little girl the world over from the time they are born? For that matter, in every little boy too."

He was silent for a time, letting Reggie and me think about his question. When he saw we didn't know the answer, he explained, "She knows that she is beautiful because her Shepherd has told that her she is beautiful. She knows who she is and that she is valuable because of the Shepherd's love for her!"

"The church I grew up in didn't teach that to little girls. We were beautiful *only* if we met certain standards and we were valuable *only* if we kept certain rules."

"I know that is the reality of how little girls are treated, but the Shepherd puts an infinite value on the Shulammite without asking for anything in return. And if you believe as I do that the Shepherd represents her Creator, then that is the answer to building confidence that sticks no matter what the circumstances. Every little girl needs to know that her Creator thinks she is beautiful inside and out."

The only thing I could think of to say was "Wow!" and I was a little embarrassed that I said it out loud and then sat there amazed at his insight. When I realized I was sitting there staring at him, I regrouped, "Now it's your turn, Caleb," inviting him to make the connection between the Shulammite and himself.

---

13. Song 1:5.

6

Enslaved by Desire

Song 6:11–12

SETTING:	In KING SOLOMON's bedroom, the SHULAMMITE remembers a nut orchard in her hometown north of Jerusalem. This flashback takes place prior to the beginning of the Song.
AT RISE:	The SHULAMMITE retells the story of being captured by KING SOLOMON's men.

SHULAMMITE

[6:11] **I went down to the nut orchard, to look at the blossoms of the valley, to see whether the vines had budded, whether the pomegranates were in bloom.** [6:12] **Before I was aware, my fancy set me in a chariot beside my prince.**[1]

---

1. Pope, *Song of Songs* 584–92, "Before I was aware, my fancy set me in a chariot" expresses her shock that she was duped into being grabbed and placed in the chariot. Her desire for fancy things had brought her too close. The word translated "fancy" literally means "soul." Some translators argue that the verse is best translated, "Before my soul was aware, I was set in a chariot."

* * *

"You see," began Caleb, "the Shulammite has been lured into becoming part of the King's harem. I too had been lured by the Grandville search committee, who painted a highly complimentary, but less than authentic picture of Grandville High for me. Obviously, they had not disclosed the ethical and moral cost of accepting the position. In fact, they were so deeply entrenched in the unjust Grandville-Rufus system that I doubt they even realized there was a cost." Caleb chuckled in advance of his own joke, "They didn't tell me that part of the job requirement was to become part of Rufus's harem. If I had known, I might've taken belly dancing lessons!"

Reggie refused to laugh, tilted his head to the side raising his eyebrows at Caleb, and then shook his head.

"Oh come on Reggie. Not only was that funny, but it's the truth of the matter too. The Shulammite had been lured away from her beloved Shepherd for a fancy chariot ride. Likewise, I had left the call that God had given me for greener grass. Both the Shulammite and I were in a miserable position."

"You said that God had given you a call?" I asked.

"For seventeen years, I had been head of the sports program at Harrelson High, my hometown high school in South Georgia. It was not a dream job by anyone else's standards. As head of the program, I coached the big sports like football and baseball. I wrestled history and science teachers into being assistant coaches in sports they knew little to nothing about. The students—many of whom were members of my father's church—well, at least their names were on the rolls—came from generations of horrific poverty. When I took that job, I had a calling to help make our community into a place where the Kingdom of God was lived out—where these kids could achieve all that their Creator meant for them to achieve."

Caleb took a sip of coffee and then went on, "But there were so many problems. Their parents were away having to work long hours in the fields. There was no money. No money for the program and no money for me. Back then, white schools got 400 percent more funding than black schools—400 percent! I was barely making my rent each month. I had no personal life. My wife had been taken by cancer five years prior and I was still wracked with her medical bills.

I had no children of my own so I was tending to my student athletes from dawn until dusk. I was their mother, their father, their teacher, and if there was enough time left over, their coach. That isn't to say there wasn't a payoff both in the sports program and in the lives of these kids. In sports, we played other black high schools and only lost on the rare occasion. I tried my best to make sports count for these boys taking every opportunity to teach them virtues and encourage strong character. I saw results, but I guess I got tired seeing most of these kids follow their parents into the fields. So when the search committee from Grandville showed up out of nowhere and offered me a job not previously open to black men, I grabbed it."

"Why was this job at Grandville suddenly open to black coaches?"

"It was 1968, the US Civil Rights Act that outlawed discrimination had been passed four years earlier. It was now illegal to discriminate in the public school system. Even though nothing much was being done to promote civil rights in the South, schools previously closed to black students and teachers were technically supposed to open their doors. Believe me, rural Georgia wasn't a bit happy about desegregation. They were simply ignoring it and on rare occasions actively fighting it. Either way there was an exception in white people's minds when it came to athletics. Out of the desire to win at sports, the white schools started making room for good black athletes. Using the same logic, they made room for a black coach too."

Caleb leaned back to pull a yearbook out of his briefcase. It was from his days at Grandville. He pointed at the pictures of Rufus and Jake, whose pictures had been taken with the athletic club. Like his son Jake, Rufus wasn't bad looking, but unlike his son, he looked professional and pulled together.

Caleb went on, "Rufus did nothing out the kindness of his heart, nor did he intend to promote civil rights. When it came to recruiting me, the most winning coach in the state, he did not discriminate. However, it wasn't because he wasn't racist. He was just using me like he used everyone else."

I stood up and walked to the window. From it, I could see the dome of the US Capitol Building. It was a jolting reminder of whose office I was standing in. "So this 'calling' to care for your young Black brothers and sisters at Harrelson, was it a calling from God?"

"It was a calling *from* and a commitment *to* God—a calling that a combination of my own greed and the half-truths of the search committee seduced me away from."

I wanted to change the subject a bit so I prompted Caleb with a statement, "Early in the Song of Solomon, the Shulammite says that her brothers were mad at her and made her work so hard that she couldn't care for herself.[2] Apparently, even before she was imprisoned in King Solomon's harem, she still faced problems. I don't suppose you have missed this correlation with your situation?"

"I haven't missed it. Her hometown community and family weren't perfect either. They didn't appreciate her as much as they should, but her beloved Shepherd *was* perfect and loved her perfectly. Her hometown was far superior to living in a harem, but it wasn't her hometown that she longed for—it was her Shepherd."

"Would it be safe to say that taking this job made you long—not so much for your hometown and family—but for God?"

"Yes. The temptation was to romanticize my hometown and old job, but it was the longing to be back doing the work God had given me to do instead of pursuing my own selfish desires that burned inside of me."

"So if the search committee seduced you into their chariot, then who does Rufus represent?"

"He is Solomon. Over the years, I have developed a theory. Rufus and Solomon, although both are real people, they are also archetypes. They are whom I call 'the oppressor.' The oppressor shows up just about anywhere human communities exist. They can be male or female. Although it is usually subtle, they are against God and humanity. The only people they are for are themselves. The oppressor's goal is to orchestrate the demise of others by seducing them away from God. He or she often works behind the scenes offering worldly pleasures—like prestige, wealth, or sex. The oppressor seduces his or her victims with flattery and gifts, but has no real love for them. Then, inevitably, as soon as the oppressor seduces the victims, the victims are left to flounder unwanted. It is the conquest that the oppressor wants. Once you are under control, you aren't interesting. The oppressor has no love or compassion for those they conquer. And in the end, the oppressor destroys them. The key to the entire operation is to destroy humanity's connection with God. Once that connection is broken, the oppressor takes God's place. But instead of being loving and nurturing like God, the oppressor sucks the life out of them."

Once again, I was slightly taken aback by Caleb's take on good and evil—though he didn't actually use the word evil. His description of the oppressor seemed a little out there—maybe a little paranoid. Yet, I could tell that Caleb was anything but paranoid. I probed more by throwing out

2. Song 1:6.

another statement, "I remember a story about a snake seducing Eve with promises that she would be like God."[3]

Caleb snapped his finger indicating that I was getting it. "The story of Adam and Eve is the earliest and most primitive story of how humanity is seduced by the oppressor, who in their case was a snake! They are seduced into an unjust system by being told that being creatures cared for by their Creator is not enough! They believe the lie that they deserve to be like their Creator. When they begin to participate in the unjust system (aligning themselves with the oppressor's wishes by eating the fruit that God has forbidden them to eat), they trade in their connection with God. And God is forced to send them away."

"Which characters are Hallie, Jake, and the school administrators?"

"They are the harem and the eunuchs. They have been enslaved by Rufus and they have bought hook, line, and sinker into his system. See, with the oppressor there always comes an unjust system. The unjust system, like the oppressor, is intrinsically against humanity. It too tries to strip humanity of its relationship with God. Grandville, like many communities, was an unjust system of its own. And like many unjust systems, they may have the appearance of idyllic life on the surface, but beneath that exterior, those caught in it are enslaved. Grandville was enslaved to Rufus. He owned them. Adam and Eve became enslaved to the broken world that the snake cracked into being. Instead of being free to live in God's Eden, they were now forced to work the earth. They no longer owned the earth that God had freely given them—it owned them."

Caleb stood up to stretch his legs. He walked over to the window where I was standing and leaned against the frame. I could tell he wanted to emphasize what he was going to say next.

"The girls in the harem had bought into Solomon's concubine system and let it define them. In fact, the whole kingdom had bought into Solomon's system—the system that says it is okay for the ruler of a nation to have sex slaves. No one even questioned it. The women, who this system affected and hurt the most, had accepted the lies that the oppressor had told them. They believed that they must be beautiful and flattering to amount to anything. So they tried to please Solomon to gain his attention. But because Solomon had already seduced them, he was no longer interested in them. He liked the chase, not what he had already conquered. In typical fashion, he turned his interest to the newest addition to the harem, the Shulammite,

3. Gen 3.

but the Shulammite is going to fight him. She may be black, she may be poor, she may have been mistreated by her family, she may have been seduced into making the mistake of getting into his chariot, she may waffle back and forth, but, in the end, she will not let this unjust system define her. She will resist the oppressor and his unjust system. And she will win by saying yes to the Shepherd."

Caleb watched Marine One lift above the trees lining the mall and turn toward the south. "There goes POTUS," he pointed out to me and then continued his explanation. "In the same way that the snake seduced Eve away from her relationship with God, the Shulammite has been seduced away from her Shepherd and placed in the harem. There was likely nothing she could have done to prevent her kidnapping, but she blames herself. Solomon will try to seduce her further until she is fully committed while the harem will also participate in trying to make her conform. They will manipulate her with a crafty collection of both truths and lies about herself."

Caleb stopped, looked me squarely in the eye, and said, "I was the Shulammite. I had been seduced into the harem. And I had to decide if I would resist the oppressor or become part of Rufus's unjust system."

"You said resist—not fight?"

"And I said it intentionally. She does not fight—there is no violence—no escape in the night—no trickery. Just peaceful resistance."

Reggie had been quiet, but that didn't mean that he wasn't engaged. He glanced at Caleb with raised eyebrows. The two had an excellent working relationship. Caleb interpreted Reggie's expression and swung his hand from Reggie to me as if to say, "You're free to tell her anything."

"We talk a lot about oppressors and unjust systems in this office. We find ourselves working toward dismantling them all of the time. At first, I thought Congressman Morgan was a little too religious and this theory of what was happening on a spiritual level in the world, a little too mystical. But I have come to understand that there are many oppressors and many unjust systems that control and enslave others. From unjust governments and economic systems to careers and relationships that hold us in bondage. You can usually identify an unjust system because it is complicated, bureaucratic, and gaudy. The Shulammite is simple, not complex, not made up. Her relationship with the Shepherd is straightforward not based on intrigue and manipulation. She is the opposite of one of the girls in the harem and the lowly Shepherd is the opposite of King Solomon. Along those lines, I have come to see a politician's role (along with other leaders' roles—clergy,

67

teachers, etc.) to be one that identifies these systems and dismantles them so that communities and individuals can thrive. Breaking down these unjust systems is the work of people of faith."

"But aren't we all part of some unjust system? I haven't found anything in this world to be perfect yet. Isn't it simply that some systems are superior to others?"

Reggie nodded, "I can't disagree with you. As humans, we will always have room to improve. However, we don't usually even see the systems that we're caught up in, much less move to fix them. For instance, we see someone who is hungry and we have been trained to think that their hunger is due to some failure on their part. But in reality, hunger is engineered by an unjust system. There is enough food to feed everyone in the world once and then have one and a half times that amount left over, but the oppressor keeps food from those who can't pay the price the oppressor wants for it."[4] It is the job of the followers of Christ to see this unjust system for what it is and work to dismantle it until no one ever goes hungry. We won't do it perfectly, but we can keep improving over time."

Reggie hesitated to go on, then made the leap, "What I am about to say next makes me cringe because I am going to sound like a Bible thumping preacher. However, the oppressor is going to insure that his harem will fight the dismantling of injustice alongside of him with greed and hatred toward anyone who gets in their way. Greedy desires for fancy things. Hatred of the poor and those who are different."

His words rang of truth. He went on to quote Jesus:

> If you belonged to the world, the world would love you as its own.
> Because you do not belong to the world, but I have chosen you out
> of the world—therefore the world hates you. (John 15:19)

"'The world will hate you!' Sure makes it sound dangerous to oppose an unjust system."

"It is," Caleb chuckled. "When we met in the airport, you asked if we were going to be doing espionage. I said no. But we're going to be under spiritual attack. It won't make the oppressor happy that we're teaching people to dismantle unjust systems. Are you ready?"

Our Sunday morning session was over. We set up our next appointment and I thanked both men while they thanked me. I felt a little silly

---

4. These are correct statistics as of the publishing of this book. The latest statistics on hunger can be found at http://www.stophungernow.org.

for we were forming a sort of mutual admiration society and I didn't feel I deserved to be admired. However, I floated home on a cloud of euphoria. This meeting—like those that were to come—felt holy. For me, a woman who had ignored God for a long time now, I was actually feeling open to the possibility of God's presence in my life.

Discerning Unjust Systems

The harem, where women were enslaved for the King's use, was an example of an unjust system accepted by society. The Shulammite's family system, where the Shulammite's brothers overworked her, was another example of an unjust system in which society agreed that it was acceptable for brothers to subjugate a sister. There were other unjust systems at work there too. One said beauty made a woman more valuable and one said black skin was not as prized as white skin.

In the Epistle of James, James writes, "Keep oneself unstained by the world."[1] Christians become stained by the world when they accept unjust systems as the way things should be. The Shulammite's society had become stained by the world because they had accepted slavery and the subjugation of women as the way things were meant to be.

It is likely that we are all caught up in unjust systems in our own culture where we are blinded to things that hurt others and, in turn, break the heart of the Good Shepherd. The goal in practicing the discipline of Discerning Unjust Systems is to train our minds to identify unjust systems and their impact on those who are caught up in them.

1. Jas 1:27.

How to Practice Discerning Unjust Systems

Day 1–2

Ask God to show you where you have been stained by the world—where you are either willingly or unwillingly participating unjust systems. Name and describe these systems in your journal. Is there an oppressor who can be named behind these systems? Name and describe the oppressor in your journal (sometimes the oppressor is not a particular person, but more of a persona). Is there a harem or eunuchs? Name and describe them.

Day 3–4

The harem did several things that harassed the Shulammite when she did not willingly conform to the unjust system. They made her feel uncomfortable about the color of her skin. They mocked her because she preferred her poor, lowly Shepherd to the rich, powerful King. Look back at the list you made on day 1 and 2. Ask God to show you how the unjust systems that you identified during day 1–2 attempt to get you to conform. Note what works on you—where are you weakest. Journal.

Day 5

The Shulammite resists the temptation to conform to the unjust harem system by first talking to her seemingly absent Shepherd and laying out what is going on: "The king has brought me into his chambers" (1:4). Then she asks the Shepherd for help: "Draw me after you, let us make haste" (1:4). Ask God to show you how you might resist the unjust systems that want to control you. Journal.

ACT 2

Solomon, the Oppressor

Then he said to me, "These are they who have come out of the great ordeal; they have washed their robes and made them white in the blood of the Lamb. For this reason they are before the throne of God, and worship him day and night within his temple, and the one who is seated on the throne will shelter them. They will hunger no more, and thirst no more; the sun will not strike them, nor any scorching heat; for the Lamb at the center of the throne will be their shepherd, and he will guide them to springs of the water of life, and God will wipe away every tear from their eyes."

—Revelation 7:14–17

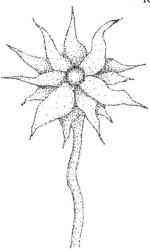

7

Solomon's Bedroom

Song 1:9—2:6

SETTING: KING SOLOMON's luxurious bedroom suite inside his
             palace in Jerusalem. The EUNUCHS responsible for the
             concubines have made certain that the SHULAMMITE
             has been appropriately bathed, perfumed, dressed, and
             decorated with jewelry for her first meeting with KING
             SOLOMON.[1]

AT RISE: KING SOLOMON is sitting on his ornate couch. The
             EUNUCHS bring the SHULAMMITE in.

KING SOLOMON

[1:9] **I compare you, my love, to a mare among Pharaoh's chariots.[2]**
[1:10] **Your cheeks are comely with ornaments, your neck with strings of jewels.** [1:11] **We will make you ornaments of gold, studded with silver.**

---

1. Esth 2:12–17 has a description of the preparation a woman went through in the ancient world to be with a king.

2. Pope, *Song of Songs*, 339. Comparing her to a horse is more of a compliment than it might sound to the modern reader. In the time of King Solomon, the Egyptian Pharaohs were known for the powerful stallions that they would take into battle. However, their enemies had discovered that mares in heat were the stallions' Achilles heel. Enemies had begun releasing mares onto the battlefield in order to make the stallions uncontrollable. King Solomon was telling her that her sex appeal was irresistible.

SHULAMMITE

(The SHULAMMITE speaks to her beloved SHEPHERD as if he were in the room.)

[1:12] **While the king was on his couch, my nard gave forth its fragrance.**[3] **[1:13] My beloved is to me a bag of myrrh that lies between my breasts.**[4] **[1:14] My beloved is to me a cluster of henna blossoms in the vineyards of En-gedi.**[5]

KING SOLOMON

[1:15] **Ah, you are beautiful, my love; ah, you are beautiful; your eyes are doves.**[6]

SHULAMMITE

(The SHULAMMITE continues to ignore KING SOLOMON and resumes talking to her absent Shepherd.)

[1:16] **Ah, you are beautiful, my beloved, truly lovely. Our couch is green;** [1:17] **the beams of our house are cedar, our rafters are pine.**[7] [2:1] **I am a rose of Sharon, a lily of the valleys.**

---

3. Pope, *Song of Songs,* 347. The word translated "couch" refers to a long low upholstered bench without a back or arms.

4. Walton et al., *The IVP Bible Background Commentary: Old Testament,* 576–77. In this verse and in the one prior, she describes a perfume satchel worn around the neck that was popular in the ancient Middle East. Because pure nard was expensive, it was probably given to her by the eunuchs as part of her preparation to meet the King. Myrrh was one of the cosmetic treatments named in Esth 2:12–17 that was used to prepare a woman for the king. The fragrance of the perfume has the unexpected result of reminding her of her beloved Shepherd.

5. En-gedi is an oasis in the desert wilderness situated on the shore of the Dead Sea.

6. Coleman, "Birds," 676–7. According to Gen 8:11, a dove was released from Noah's ark after the flood to see if the waters had receded. When the dove came back carrying an olive branch, this was a symbol of peace between God and humanity. Ever since that story, the dove has been seen as a symbol of peace. Wrapped around the Shulammite is the image of peace. Her name is very close to the word Shalom, which means peace. Later in Song 8:10, the Shulammite will state that Solomon saw her as one who brought peace. Here Solomon sees peace in her eyes.

7. A better translation might be "Our couch is the verdant grass; our walls are cedar trees and our roof is the pine tree above us." The Shulammite was comparing what she and her Shepherd had—nothing more and nothing less than creation—to the fancy palace of Solomon. She believed that what she had with her Shepherd was far superior to

KING SOLOMON

[2:2] As a lily among brambles, so is my love among maidens.[8]

SHULAMMITE

[2:3] As an apple tree among the trees of the wood, so is my beloved among young men. With great delight I sat in his shadow, and his fruit was sweet to my taste.[9] [2:4] He brought me to the banqueting house, and his intention toward me was love.[10] [2:5] Sustain me with raisins, refresh me with apples; for I am faint with love. [2:6] O that his left hand were under my head, and that his right hand embraced me![11]

(KING SOLOMON gives up. The EUNUCHS return the SHULAMMITE to the HAREM.)

***

The following morning, the athletic director dropped by Caleb's office to let him know that the two of them were going to visit Rufus. It was early February. Baseball tryouts had already taken place before Caleb had started his new job and spring practice was getting started. The athletic director pretended that the field trip to Rufus's office was a voluntary invitation, but Caleb could clearly see that it was not optional. Hobnobbing with Rufus was going to be a requirement of his job.

---

the wealth of King Solomon.

8. A better translation might be "As a lily among brambles, so are you my dear." The King was telling the Shulammite that the other women in the harem are nothing more than brambles, but that she is a lily. This is one verse where the "Solomon as a picture of God" interpretation fails since God is unlikely to whisper in our ears, "You are so much better than the rest of the humans I have created."

9. Pope, *Song of Songs*, 372–4. Gregory of Nyssa saw Christ in this apple tree. He said that Christ became one of the trees in the forest of humanity; yet, he was different from the other trees in that he offered his fruit to us. Gregory of Nyssa saw this verse as an allusion to the Eucharist. In addition, to sit in someone's shadow meant he or she was big enough to protect you. It was similar to saying, "I rest in your protection."

10. "His intention toward me was love" is literally translated "His banner over me was love." Ps 60:4 describes the banner of God: "You have set up a banner for those who fear you, to rally to it out of bowshot." The banner signified a place of safety from harm. The Shulammite is saying that her Shepherd provides a place of safety in the midst of her struggle—a place where she is truly loved.

11. She longs to feel loved, supported, and protected by her Beloved.

Rufus's office complex was nothing short of astounding. They entered into a glass and steel beamed hall that connected the two buildings that held the offices on one side and common rooms on the other. In the courtyard between the two buildings was a spectacular garden complete with a circle of standing stones reminiscent of ancient Scotland. Each stone was carefully crafted to appear aged with hand-engraved Gaelic symbols. As they walked through the halls to the meeting room where the receptionist said Rufus was waiting, the athletic director explained that Rufus was an expert in and lover of all things Scottish. No one knew exactly why Rufus had this obsession. His surname might have been Scottish, but everyone knew that his family had arrived in Georgia back in the eighteenth century as former inmates of an English debtor's prison who were being resettled in the new world. In fact, they had been one of the first settlers of the well-planned utopian experiment known as Georgia. Sadly, the utopian part quickly came to an abrupt end due to land inequities. Each settler had been given fifty acres to farm, but some of the distributed plots were un-farmable. Rufus's family had gotten lucky with good land. Then, they held on long enough for slavery to become legal in Georgia, giving them the additional advantage of slave labor. In the end, they had owned one of the largest slave plantations in the South.

As the athletic director and Caleb neared the meeting room, they could hear heated voices. The athletic director touched Caleb's arm and motioned for him to stop and keep quiet. Rufus was reading someone the riot act. "Even the devil is too smart to work like you do!" Then even louder, "Would it hurt you to have some common sense?" Undiscernible words in a different male voice followed.

Together the athletic director and Caleb stood in the hall eavesdropping. This behavior was an embarrassment to Caleb. But having no control over the situation, he stepped back a few feet and stood a yard behind the athletic director, who was straining forward to make out what was being said. The athletic director turned back to Caleb and mouthed the words, "That's Wade. He's a thug." There was a break in the heated discussion and the athletic director announced their arrival from the hall.

"Rufus, is that you?"

Both Rufus and Wade stepped from the room into the hall. Rufus showed no indication that he had been engaged in an argument, ignoring Wade's presence entirely. He had a big smile on his face and graciously welcomed Caleb. Wade's face, on the other hand, looked as though it was in a permanent frown. He offered no gesture of acknowledgement, but instantly turned away from the men and headed down the hall toward the back exit.

Wade was Rufus's "stupid" son-in-law. Rufus's daughter had divorced the then pastor of the big Southern Baptist church just a year into their marriage after catching him with his secretary. She had so desperately wanted children that she literally married the next man she met. To Rufus's disgust, that man was Wade. Wade's saving grace was that he quickly sired several beautiful granddaughters. Had this not been the case, Rufus might have done away with him.

Though Wade appeared to be of normal intelligence, he was not. In some, the lack of intelligence manifests itself as a goofy harmless persona, but not in Wade. In Wade, his frustration at not understanding the world around him enough to be able to compete in it oozed out in violent tendencies. The rumor was that he had even choked his daughters' new puppy in a fit of rage. One would have thought Rufus might have seen Wade's uncontrolled passion as a danger to his daughter and granddaughters, but like everything else, Rufus figured out a way to harness it. Wade's violent tendencies were what made him invaluable to Rufus. Rufus could count on him to take care of any dirty business that needed doing.

This arrangement was another one of those things that everyone in town knew about and everyone in town looked the other way. In fact, there were a lot of things going on in this town that the townspeople refused to acknowledge—perhaps out of fear, but more likely, because the benefit of Rufus bankrolling community projects and providing jobs outweighed his improprieties.

Rufus enthusiastically ushered the men into the meeting room and offered them sparkling water. He limped only slightly when he walked. The meeting room had two floor-to-ceiling picture windows that looked out into the courtyard. Between the windows was an enormous rock fireplace. The furniture in the room was upholstered with the Bennett Clan tartan designed specifically for Rufus by a prestigious Scottish tartan designer. He made a point of showing the men that the sparkling water was imported from an ancient source in the Scottish Highlands. Rufus served the water in gin glasses with a slice of lime. As he poured the drinks, he never stopped heaping on the praise for Caleb's career in the American Football League, his coaching successes at Harrelson, and all the great things he was going to mean for the sports programs at Grandville.

During the conversation, Rufus inquired into where Caleb was living. When Caleb told him the name of the all brick, six-unit, no frills apartment complex, Rufus groaned and looked over his half-glass spectacles at the athletic director sternly.

"We need to set Caleb up better than that." Rufus named a gated community in town and told the athletic director to get Caleb set up there and he would cover the difference in rent.

As planned, that gesture got Caleb's attention and instantly improved his impression of Rufus. Nothing like this ever happened at Harrelson. The only perks he had ever gotten were when someone's grandmother would make him a peach pie. That thought made him a little homesick, but still—a nice apartment! He could afford to buy a peach pie. Maybe things weren't so bad after all.

As Caleb was getting comfortable with Rufus, he noticed that on the mantel over the fireplace hung a huge twenty-point buck. Doc, Caleb's father, had often taken Caleb hunting. Though he had never seen a buck that big in South Georgia, he had heard they existed from time to time. The sight of the deer stirred up strong memories of home. He was reminded of the first time he saw Doc coming home from a hunt with a deer lying in the back of his truck. Caleb was new to the Morgans' house then. Doc had looked so strong that day holding up the antlers while he and Caleb posed for a picture with it. A sudden wave of both gratitude and guilt poured over him—a wave that made him once again uncomfortable with Rufus.

Next thing he knew, Caleb heard himself telling Rufus, "I am fortunate to have great memories of both my youth at Harrelson and as a coach there." The statement wasn't a lie, but it couldn't have been more disconnected from the immediate conversation. Both Rufus and the athletic director looked confused trying to figure out where Caleb was going.

Unaware of how random he sounded, Caleb continued painting Rufus a picture of Harrelson. He described his father, Doc, and the influence the old preacher had had on him. He contrasted the poverty of Harrelson with the affluence of Grandville in a way that made poverty sound good. To Rufus and the athletic director, he seemed homesick. They both wondered if he was going to resign his first week on the job. But in the end, Caleb tied it all together and explained his odd spouting of so much personal information by saying, "I would like to see my teams experience that kind of personal growth and character enrichment here at Grandville."

Immediately and without hesitation, Rufus responded, "Of course you would, Coach Morgan!"

Rufus had a way about him—a sincerity. Caleb had expected him to have horns, a tail, and a pitchfork, but instead Rufus was charming. How did this jibe with the drugs Rufus was getting for his grandson? Nothing jibed. There were layers to this situation that Caleb knew existed, but so far couldn't peel back.

As if Rufus could read Caleb's thoughts, he deftly answered Caleb's concerns, "Coach Morgan, I have debated whether or not to mention the incident my grandson told me about in the locker room. He confessed to me last night that he had been taking performance enhancing drugs himself and selling them to the other boys. We have had a long talk and I assure you that will not happen again. The boy knows what he has done was wrong. And he knows that I don't condone drug use of any kind."

To no avail, Caleb stared straight into Rufus's eyes trying hard to locate even a shadow of insincerity in them, but it wasn't there. Rufus's eyes showed what Caleb thought was a slight bit of pain in having to admit his grandson's transgressions, but Caleb could not detect anything unauthentic.

"What my grandson did has legal implications. But Coach, I would ask you not report him to the authorities. Instead, you come up with a suitable punishment and I will back you on it. It would give you a chance to help me mold my grandson and it would also save him from the legal system."

It seemed so reasonable to Caleb. No sense in getting the authorities involved. He slowly shook his head yes and suggested, "Perhaps some community service?"

"Absolutely. You arrange it and I'll make sure he does it."

Caleb was feeling comfortable again and even satisfied. He reasoned with himself that he had simply let first week jitters get a hold of him. Everything was going to be fine. He couldn't believe that he had lost sleep over this.

Then he glanced over at the athletic director. He caught a shadow, not apparent in Rufus's eyes, passing behind the eyes of the athletic director. Caleb's emotions did another one-eighty. He knew in that instant without a doubt that he was being duped. Nothing had changed. The only talk Rufus had had with his grandson was like the one he was having with Wade when they got there—to be more careful. The athletic director and Rufus were playing him for a fool.

This insight gave Caleb a renewed energy. He didn't phrase it as a challenge to Rufus, but all three men knew it was, "Rufus, I think we should look into testing the participants in the sports programs at Grandville for drugs. I was reading last night that Olympic athletes will be tested for the first time this year.[12] I need to look into it more, but from what I hear, it is an inexpensive test."

Rufus had gotten up to pour some more sparkling Scottish water for the men. His back was to them as he stood at the wet bar built discreetly into a back corner of the paneled room. Rufus didn't exactly flinch at Caleb's suggestion, but he altogether stopped moving with his back still toward the men. The room became completely quiet and for a second, no one spoke.

"Well that is an interesting approach," said the athletic director in a jolly tone, "But I don't think Grandville parents will go for that. Caleb, they are an affluent bunch. They like to think they can trust their children. Heck ninety-nine point nine percent of the time they can. Look at Rufus's grandson, for example. He told his granddaddy about the drugs on his own accord. When a student stumbles around here, parents deal with it swiftly and privately. You couldn't ask for more engaged parents or students. I assure you that drug screening is unnecessary here in Grandville."

Rufus let what the athletic director said stand and added nothing more to the conversation. He also never refilled the glasses, and instead, turned to show the men to the door. As far as Rufus was concerned, the conversation was over and so was the meeting. Caleb searched for a way to tell Rufus "No thanks" for the apartment upgrade, but there wasn't time. Rufus was done with them.

As they walked to the door, Rufus once again took up praising Caleb and welcoming him to Grandville. Rufus acted as if he was especially pleased that they had not only gotten a coach with superb coaching abilities, but one that was of strong character who could mold these young athletes into men.

When they got to the car, the athletic director smiled and said, "I think that went well." Caleb wrinkled his face in disbelief and stared at the man, who kept a pleasant look on his face, his eye on the road, and made no further summaries of the meeting. The athletic director cheerfully pointed out local landmarks to Caleb as they rode back to the gym parking lot.

Caleb was struggling to understand the differences between life in Harrelson and life in Grandville. From parenting to church, the vocabulary

12. Drug testing first took place in the 1968 Olympics in Mexico City.

was the same but they were practiced differently. Of course, there were exceptions, but in Harrelson a parent was, by definition, someone who taught their children to obey the law—not how to break it without getting caught. Similarly, in Harrelson, church by definition was a place the community went to learn the teachings of Jesus. The people of Grandville attended church too. Shoot, there was a church on every corner. But so far, he didn't see any evidence that they knew what Jesus taught.

If there were any similarities between the two towns, Harrelson loved sports as much as Grandville. And like Rufus did for his son and grandson, Caleb's parents had encouraged him to play sports in high school and college. His parents had attended every game, but unlike Rufus, they weren't obsessed with Caleb's success.

It had also not gone unnoticed by Caleb that despite their age differences, he and Rufus had a striking bit in common. Both had been athletes who had suffered disabling injuries. Caleb's neck had been fractured and Rufus had lost a leg. Both were never able to compete again. As Caleb thought about this, he was proud that his stardom during college and subsequent drafting into the AFL as a Brown didn't define him like Rufus's short-lived career had. For one thing, Negro players were only paid a fraction of what white players made so Caleb had always had to work a second job to fill in for what his paycheck didn't cover. Even if he had wanted them to be, professional sports could never have been his entire world. That explained to Caleb why his neck injury wasn't the end of his world. In fact, five years had been a long run in the AFL.

However, the loss of Rufus's leg had had a more devastating effect on Rufus. Jake had said Rufus changed, but perhaps it wasn't the loss of Rufus's leg, but the loss of Rufus's sweetheart in the accident that had changed Rufus. Caleb had lost of the love of his life too, but not until much later in life. Had the loss of his wife changed him too? It had. Caleb knew it, but he wasn't ready to admit it.

Admitting it would mean he was too much like Rufus. Admitting it would mean he would have to stop standing in judgment of Rufus. However, in the fleeting seconds that he let himself go there, he realized that their tragedies had made both of them selfish. Surely Rufus was worse—he had let his misfortune twist him into someone who was completely motivated by personal success above all else. Yet Caleb had allowed his misfortune to replace his calling with the pursuit of fancy things. Wasn't that the same thing?

Prior to coming to Grandville, Caleb had felt a spiritual calling to inspire and nurture his students. His wife and parents had been so proud of his sacrifice and desire to give back to the community. But that was seventeen years ago—five since his wife's death. He had felt the years of unending sacrifice were enough already. He wanted to be paid what he was worth for a change and work shorter hours. The Civil Rights Movement had paved the way for him to compete in the white man's world and he was going to take advantage of it. Heck, he could even talk it up. He had told everyone back home that he was venturing out into the white man's world to pave the way for others. That was the angle he took when explaining his decision to his family and friends. "I am going to be the goodwill ambassador for other Negro coaches who deserve the same opportunities as white coaches."

Neither his dad nor the elders in his dad's church bought it. Doc had put it this way, "Son, we didn't work for civil rights because we thought we should take on white America's values and goals. We worked for civil rights so we could be free to be all God created us to be—pursuing God's goals. Fulfilling our purpose and the freedom to pursue our dreams go hand in hand, but our dreams have got to be God's dreams or they aren't worth much."

This statement had led to quite a long conversation. Couldn't a Christian be rich? Didn't a Christian have a right to have nice things? Doc didn't think so—not as long as people, white or black, were in need. "It's like you're stealing from your brother and sister when you work for selfish achievements. It's slavery all over again. Slavery to the almighty dollar."

Caleb wished that he had used another angle to explain why he was taking the Grandville job. He hadn't been able to fool his dad or the church elders and it was embarrassing.

***

The three of us had gathered once again in the Cannon Office Building, but due to busy weekend schedules, we met early on a Monday morning instead of Sunday this time. Halfway through the morning, an unexpected visitor had stopped by to see Caleb so Reggie and I sat chatting about the Washington scene. I was in the process of goading Reggie into telling me whether he had a girlfriend or not when Caleb lumbered back into the room.

As I often did, I made a statement and then let Caleb evaluate its merit, "Rufus is turning out to be expert at using flattery to manipulate, but it seems to me that Rufus's flattery—so far anyway—has been true."

"Excellent observation young lady!" exclaimed Caleb as he sat back down. "Rufus's flattery was slightly over the top, but never false. This is how oppressors prefer to work. They've got no moral objection to telling outright lies, but they prefer to manipulate by telling you the truth—out of context. That way, it feels true, catches you off-guard, and subtly gets you to agree."

Reggie weighed in, "For instance, think about the creation story again. The snake told Eve the truth—she wouldn't physically die if she ate the fruit that God had told her not to eat. Nevertheless, the snake failed to mention that it was a spiritual death God was warning her against. She'd be cast out of the garden and out of relationship with God."[13]

Rufus had flattered Caleb by saying he was a person of strong character. Yet Caleb's strong character only had meaning in the context of service to God. Put Caleb in service to Rufus and his strong character, which made him a loyal team player, meant nothing. Loyalty to the oppressor was misplaced and wrong. If Caleb's talent wasn't being used in service to God, it was no longer full of meaning or purpose. Using one's talents to prop up drugged boys and send them onto the field—even if it bought Caleb things he wanted and thought he needed—was a misuse of his God-given gifts.

"But Caleb, wasn't it true that if you made the sports program at Grandville High (and Rufus's grandson) a success that it really would do something for African-American coaches in the way of showing that desegregation worked?"

"Maybe, but at the cost of becoming part of Rufus's harem. You have to understand that this story is not just about race—even though civil rights issues help make the point. It is about following the call that God had placed upon me—about doing what I was created to do—instead of letting unjust systems enslave me. And most of all it's about exposing the lie that it's okay to benefit from systems that make others suffer."

"Let me stop you for a moment. This line of thinking ties into what I have been pondering about our conversation about the Reign of God. We said that God reigns when the interests of all are met—when no one goes hungry or in need while others have more than enough."

"We did say that."

13. Gen 3.

"Well, I was watching the interview of an executive who is known to be a skilled negotiator. They asked his business partner what made this executive so skilled at making a deal. His partner said that his superpower was in convincing people to give up what was rightly theirs. He said that no one walks away from this executive's negotiating table better off. In other words, he doesn't negotiate for the win-win. He negotiates for the win-lose."

"That is the opposite of the Reign of God. The sad thing is that our society is blind to the fact that taking advantage of someone else is wrong. It is an unjust form of capitalism that prides itself in holding others down while building oneself up."

"Society rewards and admires oppressors."

"Yes, they do."

Reggie threw in another example. "Just last week, I needed a new shirt. We have been trained to think it is smart to buy the cheapest well-made shirt that we can find. However, we haven't been taught to ask if the shirt was made with just standards, if the seamstress was paid fairly, if her working conditions were humane, if her employer provided health insurance? It's a lie to think I am justified in buying a shirt made by the victim of an unjust system just because it is well made and priced cheaply. It is still wrong."

"Did you buy your shirt?"

"At a consignment store."

"Get out!" I was shocked. Reggie dressed so well.

"Yep! I didn't have time to research shirt manufacturers so I figured this was at least a sustainable option."

I needed to think about that one. Reggie really did take dismantling injustice seriously. Was I willing to take it that far?

Meanwhile, Caleb explained, "The Song teaches people to understand the hold that unjust systems have on them and how to overcome that hold."

This time Caleb asked me if *I* saw the connection to the Shulammite. In fact, I did. Solomon flattered her by saying that she was beautiful. And she was. He told her the truth about herself, but he (along with the girls in the harem) twisted that truth. They made her think that her beauty defined her and that she could to use her beauty to buy favors from the King, gaining all that she had ever wanted—power within the harem, the love of a King, and even some nice jewelry. In truth, her real needs would never be met by Solomon nor would she ever be valued for her God-given talents and gifts.

However, the Shulammite was smart. She knew that her beauty was only meaningful in the context of her beloved Shepherd. For Solomon, her beauty brought forth the lustful thoughts of a stallion toward a mare. In contrast, her Shepherd's "intentions toward her were love."[14] Not lust, but love. She resisted Solomon by calling out to the Shepherd, remembering her Shepherd, and ignoring Solomon. She ignored him, not in the sense that she let the oppressor go unchecked, but she ignored him by not allowing him to create even the tiniest bit of space for himself in her heart.

When I was done elaborating, Caleb commented, "Good point! She doesn't really ignore Solomon in the sense of pretending that he doesn't exist. She knows he is there and she seems to be the only one in the harem that knows he is a predator—an oppressor. Doc liked to quote the Apostle Paul and say, 'Don't give the devil a foothold.'[15] That is a better description of what she is doing than saying she is ignoring Solomon. She is plenty aware of who Solomon is and what he wants. She isn't pretending that he isn't there. Like you said, she is denying him any space in her heart."

"Maybe we should call her technique 'Remembering While Blocking,'" I suggested with a laugh. Then onto another subject I asked, "Why did Rufus dismiss you so quickly that afternoon? Was it simply so he wouldn't have to deal with your suggestion that students be screened for drugs?"

"That was part of it, but Rufus was *never* afraid of me. I figured out later that week that the white boy buying the amphetamines from Rufus's grandson was the chief of police's son. Rufus was not afraid of what would happen if I reported the steroid use. He simply didn't want to get off on the wrong foot by chancing an argument with me. For an oppressor like Rufus, it is all about the chase. He wanted me to hop in his pocket willingly. He wanted to buy me with flattery and gifts. And in turn, I would make his grandson a contender for a professional career in baseball."

"How did you handle the situation?"

"I did what the Shulammite did. I remembered the Shepherd and blocked the oppressor. I also vowed to stay as far away from the Bennett clan as possible. So for the next few months, I did my job and stayed out of their way."

Our time was up and it was once again time for me to leave. I decided that instead of heading straight home, I would walk over to the Library of

14. Song 2:4.
15. Eph 4:27, KJV.

Congress where I could sit in one of the majestic three-story reading rooms and make some notes about the morning's meeting.

I was intrigued that Solomon, like Rufus, was turned on by the chase and not just the act of conquering. Solomon could have raped the Shulammite, but that wasn't what he wanted. He wanted to seduce her. It was the same thing with the snake in the garden. He wooed Eve with promises, instead of force-feeding her the fruit. Is it because the oppressor and the unjust system can only have a spiritual hold on us if we *willingly* give power to them? Could it be that evil can't force us to abandon our relationship with God and that the Reign of God is more powerful than any unjust system?

The concept that Caleb had mentioned of "remembering" in order to halt temptation was interesting to me. I recalled from my time spent in Sunday school that the Hebrews strayed in the desert for forty years because they couldn't remember the last miracle God had performed and were always doubting that God controlled their future. Their doubts kept them from moving into the Promised Land time after time.[16]

Lost in my thoughts, I was jolted when a deep voice from behind me whispered two sentences as if they were one, "I don't have a girlfriend, would you like to go get a coffee?"

I couldn't help but laugh out loud. My laugh echoed through the reading room as my hand shot to cover my lips so that the sound wouldn't disturb others. "Are you stalking me again like you and Congressman Morgan did that day in the airport?"

"No. I come here often to work. Are you stalking me?"

"Now there is a good pickup line. That's why you don't have a girlfriend."

"Hmmm. How about I use one of Solomon's pickups and compare you to a horse?"

"Cute! Is there any wonder that the King couldn't win over the Shulammite? The man had no game. He compared her to animals and fruit!"

"So true! But you know who has good coffee? The atrium in the Natural History Museum."

As we walked to the museum, I told Reggie I had been thinking about what Caleb had said about "Remembering While Blocking" as a technique to steal oneself against the effects of injustice.

Reggie, knowing the Bible better than I did, pointed out that in the New Testament when Jesus broke bread with the disciples at the last supper,

---

16. Heb 3:16, 18–19; 4:1–3, 11.

he told them to "Do this in remembrance of me."[17] Reggie went on to explain, "This type of remembrance, along with the breaking of bread and sharing of wine, is an unusual sort of remembering. We not only remember what was, but what was joins itself to us in the here and now as we also remember what is promised. In this Eucharistic—or thankful—kind of remembering, we are also nourished with the body of Christ so that we can do God's will. Did you notice that the Shulammite compares him to an apple tree and says, 'his fruit was sweet to my taste?'[18] Gregory of Nyssa believed that this was a foreshadowing of Christ giving his body to us on the cross and in the Eucharist."[19]

"So you think there is something mystical about remembering what God has done and what God has promised?"

"I do. And I think there is something powerful in the taking of the bread that nourishes us with the body of Christ to do the work of God, including dismantling unjust systems."

"Was the Shulammite's intentional remembering of her Shepherd while blocking Solomon something more than just a good idea?" I wondered out loud. "Did it also nourish her in the mystical way we are nourished in the Eucharist?"

"I think so. It's also curious to me that blocking and remembering go hand in hand. Throughout the entire song, the Shulammite never answers Solomon—not directly. She turns her back on Solomon while she remembers (in audible tones) her beloved Shepherd. This act of blocking evil and remembering brings her Shepherd into her current situation although he is not there physically. It is as if she is giving her Shepherd a seat on the couch between her and the King. She simultaneously makes space for the Shepherd while she says no to the King's desires."

"Perhaps she knew that when one opens the door to negotiating with temptation, one has already lost the battle. It's a door that needs to remain shut."

"Yet, 'just saying no' doesn't work either. What works is the act of replacing the space made by blocking with remembering. In this way, the Shulammite thwarts Solomon's efforts to seduce her in the same way that Caleb thwarted Rufus's efforts."

17. Luke 22:19.

18. Song 2:13.

19. Pope, *Song of Songs*, 372–4.

Resist the Oppressor

Song 2:7

SETTING: The chambers of the KING SOLOMON's HAREM within his palace in Jerusalem.

AT RISE: The women of the HAREM have gathered to see what the SHULAMMITE thought of her first encounter with KING SOLOMON.

SHULAMMITE

(The SHULAMMITE addresses the HAREM.)

^{2:7} **I adjure you, O daughters of Jerusalem, by the gazelles or the wild does: do not stir up or awaken love until it is ready!**[1]

***

Caleb had taught me that, like Eve's struggle with the snake, unjust systems are set into motion when humans are enticed to take from others what they want instead of being satisfied with what God has provided for everyone. Though Solomon was the oppressor, the harem girls were playing

1. Ginsburg, *The Song of Songs*, 144. She will use these same words in verses 3:5 and 8:4. This chorus seems to occur after she has successfully resisted. It is as if to say to the harem, "I can resist Solomon and so can you."

into his unjust system whenever they begged for Solomon's love or competed with each other for the best spots in the harem. Yet, what Solomon gave was not love at all. It was lust at best. The Shulammite adjured the harem girls to resist. Only lust can be stirred up. Love is awakened when it is right. Her message was, "Don't compromise. You weren't created to be sex slaves. You were created to be loved." Unfortunately, as we will see later, the girls in the harem are so entrenched in this unjust system that they cannot understand that it is possible or even desirable to resist. All they understand is lust and seduction. They have no concept of being loved or of loving the King. They also have no idea that they too are loved by their Creator and have infinite worth in the Creator's eyes. This was on my mind a week later when Reggie greeted me in the lobby of the Cannon Office Building that Sunday morning. He was just arriving, as well.

"So what do you think?" he inquired.

"About what?" Did he want to know what I had thought about the previous Monday afternoon's adventure spent getting coffee together and slowly walking the halls of the museum chatting about everything from religion to politics? It was more fun than I had had in forever, but I didn't want to just blurt that out.

"About the story, about Congressman Morgan, about writing this all down and sharing it with the world."

Thankful I had asked before answering, I responded appropriately, "I'm still pinching myself that Congressman Morgan asked me to write his story. But honestly, I'm worried a bit that a lot of people may mock it. And I'm also seriously concerned that I'm not a good enough writer."

"You will do a fine job—I can promise you that." I believed Reggie meant it. He was just as genuine as Caleb was. In addition, he was one of those people who wanted to smile all the time—not because he was ignorant of the problems in world around him, but in spite of them. He was simply a happy person filled with the hope that he could make a positive impact in the world.

"They probably *will* mock it," Reggie commented as he held the elevator door for me. "Does that make you *not* want to be the author?"

"No. This may be the best thing I have ever done. My only worry is about Congressman Morgan's feelings."

"Don't worry about him. He has dealt with the world a very long time. He is a solid rock."

★ ★ ★

Back in Grandville, the rest of Caleb's first week had been calm. He was more than a little thankful for this. He had spent time getting to know his teams and the rest of the school staff. From time to time, he felt uneasy, but tried to chalk it up to homesickness. Indeed, he was homesick. Yet, deep in his heart, he knew the problem was bigger than that.

Saturday night was the Valentine's Day dance at the school. It was an occasion where the entire town was invited—not just students. It was mandatory for all of the teachers to attend as chaperones. Yet, there was some concern among the school staff as to whether Caleb ought to attend or not. On one hand, the community needed some time to get used to having a black coach and it might be advisable for him to lay low for a while—at least until after they'd had a winning season. On the other hand, the school needed all the extra hands they could get for the event. It was decided Caleb would come during setup and help with the heavy lifting, but go home before students started arriving. So much for Caleb being an icon of progress.

That morning, he showed up and was doing his part helping put the stage in place for the band. Around lunchtime, he felt a hand squeeze his bicep. It was Hallie and standing behind her was Rufus. Both had big smiles on their faces. Her smile said she was impressed with his muscular arm. Rufus's smile just said hello. Together they invited him to lunch at Hallie and Jake's place. Caleb was economical with the truth and said he already had plans. He worked about an hour and then headed to his car, feeling guilty for being so critical of Rufus and his clan. They had acted so graciously to him. Why was he being so judgmental?

The question went without answer as he dodged a close call with a pickup truck being driven by a teen. When he reached his car, which had been sandwiched between two big pickup trucks, he sat there studying the local map and thinking about how he would spend the rest of the day.

His contemplation didn't last long. A man and a woman appeared beside the passenger side door of his car. They were standing. From that angle, they couldn't see him sitting in the driver's seat. Apparently, they felt safe and private standing between the trucks parked on either side of Caleb's car. Caleb could hear them talking and recognized one of their voices. It was Jake. However, the woman with him was not Hallie. From what he could see of her, she was only half as attractive as Hallie—large boned and heavy. She was wearing a dark men's style pantsuit in contrast to the shapely dress Hallie had had on. Caleb could hear every word they said. They were obviously having an affair and she wanted to break it off. Jake didn't. In angry tones, she reminded Jake that she was single and needed a life of her own—she wanted a husband and children. Jake didn't seem to hear her. He took her hand and pushed her up against Caleb's car —a bold move in the school parking lot. She didn't resist, but the embrace lasted only a second before Jake backed off and walked away. The woman stood motionless beside Caleb's car. Her body shaking. At first, Caleb didn't realize why she was shaking. As far as he could tell, Jake hadn't hurt her. Then he realized the woman was crying.

She ran to her car several rows over and climbed into the driver's seat. She sat there, her head lowered, her red curls hiding her face. Caleb knew this was his cue to leave.

***

"So Jake was having an affair," I posited.

"Jake, like the rest of the harem, had bought into the unjust system that was telling him this was all there would ever be—that he was stuck living in his father's shadow in a family and a town that made him miserable. Instead of dealing with his situation by letting God guide him, Jake took matters into his own hands. He decided that his needs were more important than the harm he was bringing to that young woman or his wife and kids. In doing so, he settled for a lot less than God would have given him. He had traded in the possibility of love for lust."

"But is lust always wrong?" I wondered out loud. Both men laughed.

"Well. I guess it's all in how you define the word," answered Caleb. For me, lust says to the other person, "I want *you* to make *me* happy." Love says to the other person, "I want to make *you* happy." I am using the word *lust* to mean sexual desire without love. That is a recipe for abuse," Caleb responded.

"Okay. Let me summarize. The Shulammite is telling the harem that they need to reject the lustful Solomon, King of the unjust system that holds them as sex slaves, and wait for love."

"Yes. She wants them to stop calling out to Solomon begging him for attention," answered Caleb. "God, unlike Solomon, pursues humanity like the Shepherd whose intention toward us is love. Solomon, the oppressor, pursues us differently. He tries to seduce us into taking part in his unjust system. God, on the other hand, truly loves us and wants us to be set free from oppression so we can be our best selves."

Reggie interjected, "I think it's important to note that lust comes in many forms. Sex is only one of them." He gave an example from one of the congressional representative's recent initiatives—an affordable housing project in his district. Caleb had run into an organized group of what he called "slumlords" who were intent on keeping rent high by forming a pact with all of the property owners in the area. In doing so, they were making the poor even poorer. "They wanted to pad their own pockets with money obtained upon the backs of the working poor. These slumlords were trying to obtain things for themselves that God had intended for the poor to have. Theirs was the lust for money not sex."

"Yes and as badly as some scholars have wanted the Song of Solomon to be a kind of ancient sex manual, it isn't about sex. Oh, it's sexual, all right. But sex isn't the point," added Caleb.

With that, Reggie went back to naming a variety of unjust systems that were hurting humanity. "How about an industry that delivers unneeded antibiotics at the risk of making all infections immune to antibiotics? Or one that keeps affordable fresh vegetables and fruits from the inner city grocery store? Or sports that pad the owners and players' pockets, but do nothing for the working poor in the surrounding community who are displaced from their houses when the stadium is built and then forced to accept minimum wages working at the stadium? Or one that sells subpar baby formula to nursing mothers? Unjust systems always work for the oppressor at the expense of the vulnerable."

Reggie was preaching to the choir. And what Caleb had said about the difference between lust and love resonated with me. In these verses, the Shulammite was not reprimanding the Solomons of the world. The Shulammite was rallying the harem—trying to awaken victims who had bought into the system. She wanted them to realize that they deserved better and could resist Solomon as she was doing.

The harem was more complex than one might think. The King was using the concubines and they were using the King. The women may have thought that they were stuck. However, the Shulammite had demonstrated that there were ways to resist, thwarting Solomon's advances at every turn. They might not be able to escape the walls of the palace, but they didn't have to play the King's game. They could stop seeking the King's advances, they could turn down his gifts, and they could lay out their situation before God and listen for God to guide them. They could refuse to worry about their standing in the harem and focus on helping one another. They could simply refuse to play the game. They could live into the truth that their value was not found in the King's booty call.

Unlike the girls in the harem, Caleb was not physically stuck at Grandville—though it might be risky to leave without a job and embarrassing to explain. The harem, however, had physical barriers to leaving that cannot be minimized or overlooked. Yet, the Shulammite spoke to the harem of becoming spiritually free from the oppressor's hold. Spiritual freedom must happen—otherwise removing physical barriers makes no difference. Caleb had allowed the oppressor to bind him spiritually. Until he overcame this, he would never be free.

I turned to Caleb, "In the end, you refused to play the game. You refused to take part in the unjust system and to kowtow to Rufus, didn't you?"

"Come back next week—same time, same place—and see for yourself," laughed Caleb.

For me, this opened a whole new way of thinking. What unjust systems had I bought into? I thought of the church I had grown up in—one where women were not allowed to take part in the leadership. The women who attended had bought into the idea that God had sanctioned their second-class station in life. They believed that they were not smart enough or too emotional to be leaders. They didn't believe that Jesus had reconciled them to God in the complete way that God had reconciled their husbands to God. Perhaps, like the Shulammite, it was my duty to call out to them "by the gazelles and the wild does" not to accept that unjust system, but to come fully alive in the Good Shepherd's love.

I could see why Caleb wanted a woman to write his story—and why it did not matter to him that I was white. The Shulammite's story spoke to everyone regardless of race or sex.

Eucharistic Remembrance

The Shulammite practiced Eucharistic Remembrance (or Thankful Remembrance) when a scent from her perfume satchel reminded her of her Shepherd. Remembering allowed her to avoid the temptation to give in to King Solomon's desires. However, there are many examples in the Bible where the lack of remembering has the opposite effect.

For instance, God provided safe passage for the Israelites by miraculously parting the Red Sea, but not long afterwards, they were overcome with worry and faithlessness about where their next meal would come from.[1] Certainly, a God who can part the Red Sea can provide food, but somehow they had already forgotten about God's power. This kind of faithlessness that comes from forgetfulness is always coupled with ungratefulness. Humanity, instead of remembering and being thankful for God's blessings, seems to be constantly asking God, "What have you done for me lately?" when what we truly need to do to is to thankfully remember what God has done in the past and then rest in the fact that God loves us and will continue to provide for us.

The most important example of thankful remembrance in scripture happens on the night that Jesus was arrested. "He took a loaf of bread, and when he had given thanks, he broke it and gave it to them, saying, 'This is my body, which is given for you. Do this in remembrance of me'" (Luke 22:19). This was the first celebration of the Eucharist.

1. Exod 16:1–2.

How to pray the Prayer of Eucharistic Remembrance

Jesus taught us by example at the Last Supper to give thanks and to remember. The Shulammite and Caleb both spoke aloud their thankful remembrance in the presence of the oppressor in order to fight their temptation. Their thankfulness served to discourage the temptations they were facing. Each day this week, focus on either collective memories of God found in Scripture or your own memories. Suggestions for each day are given below. Start by asking God to reveal God's self in these memories, then meditate on them. Remember what God has done, who God is, and give thanks. Journal.

Day 1

Read John 11:1–45, The Resurrection of Lazarus.

Day 2

Remember how God provided for you in your childhood.

Day 3

Read Matt 17:24–27, Finding the Money to Pay Taxes.

Day 4

Remember how God has provided for you in your adult life.

Day 5

Read Mark 5:1–20, The Healing of the Demoniac.

ACT 3

The Good Shepherd

"I am the good shepherd. The good shepherd lays down his life for the sheep. The hired hand, who is not the shepherd and does not own the sheep, sees the wolf coming and leaves the sheep and runs away—and the wolf snatches them and scatters them. The hired hand runs away because a hired hand does not care for the sheep. I am the good shepherd. I know my own and my own know me, just as the Father knows me and I know the Father. And I lay down my life for the sheep. I have other sheep that do not belong to this fold. I must bring them also, and they will listen to my voice. So there will be one flock, one shepherd.

—John 10:11–16

9

The Shulammite Sends the Shepherd Away
Song 2:8–17

SETTING: KING SOLOMON's country estate located in the Northern Kingdom in or near Lebanon. It is also near Shulem,
the SHULAMMITE's hometown. The SHULAMMITE
has been taken along with other members of the HA-
REM to the country estate in preparation for the King's
arrival.

AT RISE: The SHULAMMITE is in the HAREM's bedroom when
she hears the far off voice of her SHEPHERD. Other
members of the HAREM are around, but they pay no attention to what the SHULAMMITE is doing. She peers
out of her bedroom window into the hills. She is ecstatic
that her SHEPHERD has found her.

SHULAMMITE

2:8 **The voice of my beloved! Look, he comes, leaping upon the mountains, bounding over the hills.** 2:9 **My beloved is like a gazelle or a young
stag. Look, there he stands behind our wall, gazing in at the windows,
looking through the lattice.** 2:10 **My beloved speaks and says to me . . .**

SHEPHERD

Arise, my love, my fair one, and come away; [2:11] for now the winter is past, the rain is over and gone.[1] [2:12] The flowers appear on the earth; the time of singing has come, and the voice of the turtledove is heard in our land.[2] [2:13] The fig tree puts forth its figs, and the vines are in blossom; they give forth fragrance. Arise, my love, my fair one, and come away. [2:14] O my dove, in the clefts of the rock, in the covert of the cliff, let me see your face, let me hear your voice; for your voice is sweet, and your face is lovely. [2:15] Catch us the foxes, the little foxes, that ruin the vineyards—for our vineyards are in blossom.[3]

SHULAMMITE

[2:16] My beloved is mine and I am his; he pastures his flock among the lilies. [2:17] Until the day breathes and the shadows flee, turn, my beloved, be like a gazelle or a young stag on the cleft mountains.[4]

***

Caleb coached and tried to get acclimated to Grandville as the months went by. The gentle rolling countryside was an interesting contrast to the flat southern plains where he had grown up. Both were beautiful in their own way. Despite their beauty, he was more depressed and lonesome than he had ever been in his life. He came to realize that most of the students and their families were oblivious to how things were run in the town and in the

1. The Shepherd sings a type of resurrection chorus or "Spring Song" that he will repeat again later: "Arise and come away!" He not only tells her how spring is being birthed from the dead of winter, but he invites her to follow him to freedom.

2. The turtledove was a migratory bird whose appearance announced that spring had arrived.

3. Exum, *Song of Songs,* 129. Foxes do not eat grapes. Most likely foxes disturbed the ancient middle-east vineyards by burrowing into the ground and damaging the roots of the grape vines. The point that the Shepherd is making is that the "little" pests are the worst kind of pest. You could likely catch a big animal trampling a vineyard, but these little foxes were sneaking in undetected. The Shepherd is warning her to take nothing for granted and not to succumb to the seemingly insignificant challenges before her.

4. The Shulammite pledges her love to the Shepherd, but then sends him away. She believes that he is going to get caught in the broad daylight and that he needs to go away until it is safe. She is worried for their safety. She has forgotten that not only is the Shepherd fearless, but he is also powerful.

school. They went about their daily lives generally unaware of how deeply the Bennett family's antics influenced their community. They saw the Bennetts as an asset to their town and willingly went along with whatever they wanted.

It was May before Caleb knew it and baseball playoffs were wrapping up. He wasn't taking it personally that the team didn't get very far in the playoffs. He hadn't been on board in time for tryouts or pre-season practices, but now that he had been with the boys for several months, he was in a good place to assess their skills and make things happen the following year.

To his relief, he had also been able to avoid the Bennetts as much as was reasonable given Rufus was at every practice and game. He heard nothing more about (nor had he seen any evidence of) drugs being sold or used at the high school. Rufus was beyond pleased with how he felt his grandson was maturing into the sport, which meant that he couldn't have been happier with Caleb. It went unspoken what everyone including Caleb knew. While Rufus's grandson was good, he wasn't great. If the kid wanted to be great, he had a lot of work to do. He would need to put on muscle and height that only genetics could generate and he would need to toughen up mentally. In truth, Caleb was far from certain that the boy had any chance of ever making it to the big leagues.

Furthermore, what loomed under the seemingly tranquil surface was that Caleb had two boys on the team who were more developed athletes than Rufus's grandson. They not only had raw talent, but the mental and emotional fortitude to be phenomenal players. Caleb had an unwelcome choice before him. Would he put the team before promoting Rufus's grandson and give these boys the opportunities they had earned and deserved? Or would he do what was best for himself and make Rufus happy? One way they would win and the deserving players would have the opportunity to demonstrate their talents. The other way he would keep his job. For now, at least until the fall scrimmages started, all he had to do was coast. Until he got a call from his old stomping ground.

"Caleb!" the caller sounded happy. It took Caleb a few seconds to recognize the voice on the other end. It was one of the young science teachers at Harrelson. The two of them chatted about the latest gossip back home, talked about the caller's family, and then the caller got around to asking what he had called to ask.

"Caleb, what would you think about our two schools having a summer scrimmage? I know segregation is still a hot issue, but I thought if those folks at Grandville hired a black coach, maybe they'd be willing to play a black high school."

Caleb wanted to quickly put an end to this idea, but before he could, the caller went on, "I know how important desegregation in sports is to you, so I thought it might be fun and could send a positive message."

"Oh I don't know," replied Caleb. But in reality, Caleb knew. Caleb knew that the administration and parents at Grandville would never let their sons travel to a black high school for a game. He also knew they darn well wouldn't let a black team come to Grandville to play. The only reason Caleb didn't say no immediately was that he was embarrassed to admit that his leaving Harrelson had not actually—so far anyway—been helpful in promoting civil rights. To outsiders, he knew that he still looked like a guy who was making steps forward for social justice, but if he told the truth—that the people at Grandville were every bit as racist as anywhere else in the state—then it would be obvious that he had given up his ministry to Harrelson kids for his own pocketbook.

Instead of coming clean, Caleb said, "I'll talk to the athletic director and see what he thinks." Caleb hung up and decided to wait a few days and phone with an excuse. Pursuing this idea with anyone at Grandville would have been ridiculous.

However, over the next few days, his conscience got the better of him. He didn't want "lying to his hometown buddies" to go on his list of missteps. Therefore, he found himself sitting in the sparse office of the athletic director one more time looking at the photo of the man's wife and son. Caleb flippantly presented the idea fully expecting to be immediately turned down, but to his surprise, the athletic director pursed his lips and slowly shook his head up and down thoughtfully.

"Interesting," he mumbled, as he stretched out staring at the ceiling. "If I'm not wrong, we've scrimmaged with a white school near Harrelson just last year—isn't Williamson High near Harrelson?"

Caleb shook his head yes.

The athletic director went on, "Rufus . . ." Oh how Caleb hated hearing that name. He could live the rest of his life and never hear that name again. What now? "Rufus has a hunting estate down there. I don't know if you were aware of that. His family is from that area and he spent summers there as a kid. He has contacts in the sports department at Williamson. Even arranged the scrimmage himself. We beat'em too! What if we borrowed their field and met on neutral turf?"

"Afraid to send white people into the black neighborhood?" jabbed Caleb.

"Some things aren't meant to change, Caleb. Let me run this by Rufus and see if he wants to arrange it. It would be sort of fun to see you up against your own people!" The athletic director's last words, "Up against your *own* people," rang in Caleb's ears.

Remarkably, Rufus arranged everything. He warned Caleb that some parents might not let their sons play in the scrimmage and to just let them be. The team would play with whomever showed up.

The game was to take place in mid-July. As the date grew closer, Rufus stopped by the high school to visit with Caleb. "Looking forward to the game," Rufus announced as he entered Caleb's office. "I was thinking this may be a first in Georgia—a white school playing an all-black high school."

"A *mostly* white school" corrected Caleb. He continued without waiting for a reaction from Rufus, "Could be. I don't know of any other schools that have done this."

"Let's get some publicity on this. It'd be good for the up-and-coming players. I'm going to contact a friend in the sports department at the Atlanta Journal. I think they'd be interested in covering it."

"More likely the Constitution would cover it than the Journal," snapped Caleb with a tone of disgust just barely hidden from Rufus. Caleb was irritated enough with the situation at Grandville that he had started poking at Rufus and his harem every chance he got. He knew that wasn't smart, but he couldn't seem to help himself. The Constitution was the liberal side of the Atlanta newspaper, whereas the Journal was known to be notoriously one-sided and conservative.

"Do you know someone at the Constitution?" Rufus inquired.

"No. But the editors at the Journal aren't going to get excited about a scrimmage between a black and a white school."

"Leave it to me," insisted Rufus with a pride that said he had everything under control. "Have you had any students back out?"

"Not yet."

"Good," declared Rufus. "I had a school board meeting this morning and thought I would stop by. I can't tell you how much I appreciate all the hours you have been putting in with the team. You're bringing out the best in our boys. Next year is going to be astounding."

"Thank you," responded Caleb without looking at Rufus. Caleb hated talking to Rufus so much that at that moment he couldn't even force himself to make eye contact.

"I have a hunting lodge down in Colquitt County that isn't being used right now. Why don't you take a day off before the game and head on down there? You could have the boathouse to yourself if you went down ahead of us on Thursday. I think you'd find it renewing to the body and soul. There's a lake on the property with a shack by the boathouse full of fishing poles. I know moving must have been stressful and this would give you some time to kick back. The team will arrive Friday afternoon for practice, of course, but you'd still get to enjoy a day of well-deserved downtime. Jake, Hallie, and myself will come down on Saturday for the game and spend Saturday night. But we'd expect you to stay with us. What do you say?"

Inviting a black man to stay with a white family was not done—even if the invitation was for the boathouse. Right and wrong always became fuzzy when Rufus was around. Caleb momentarily couldn't remember why he was supposed to turn down the offer, but remembered that he should. "Very generous of you, but I was planning to stay with my folks."

Ignoring Caleb's refusal, Rufus continued, "Feel free to invite them out to visit you before we arrive. Maybe have your dad out to fish Friday morning."

Caleb wanted to say yes and Caleb wanted to say no. He needed a vacation badly, "What the heck. Thank you, I'd love to!"

"Great! I'll send the keys over."

Several weeks later, when time for the big game arrived, Caleb drove home to Colquitt County to take advantage of Rufus's offer. He stopped first at Rufus's lodge to drop off his things and check the place out. It was rustic in design, but catered to every luxury. The grounds were enormous, private, and beautiful. The air was filled with the smell of pine needles. Caleb opened up the boathouse, drove out to see his parents, and invited them to come fishing with him the following day.

His parents had a small yellow house with a big front porch at the end of a street lined with identical homes each painted a unique color. There he sat with his dad in the front porch swing that Doc had built for his mom. Neighbors passed by and stopped to chat. But mostly, the street was very quiet with only an occasional bird's song or squirrel's chattering. After a while they went inside. It was good to see his mom, sit at her kitchen table, and hear her talk away about all that was going on in town.

His mother had a small garden outside her kitchen. After a while, the phone rang and she went to get it while he wandered outside to see what was growing. He couldn't help but see the hand of God at work in the little garden in a way that he hadn't been quiet enough to experience in a long time. When had he last felt this content and close to God? He couldn't remember. Grabbing a few minutes alone, he sat down on the concrete stoop drinking his mother's sweet tea straight from a gallon jug that had once held milk. He listened to the stillness in a world that he had forgotten. He imagined if he was quiet enough, he might even hear God speak.

Eventually, he wandered to the hammock in the backyard. He may have fallen in and out of sleep. Unexpectedly, he was suddenly aware of movement near him. It was a young buck not more than a dozen feet from where he lay. It was common for deer to venture into the neighborhood from the surrounding farmlands. He was enticed by the creature—almost jealous of him. The buck was free to be who God had created him to be. It didn't desire fame and fortune. It just lived off of God's creation. The more he thought about it, the more Caleb wanted nothing more than to be that buck. The more he thought about that, the angrier he grew at his circumstances. He was angry with the search committee, angry with Rufus, angry with the school staff. Wretchedly, he also remembered that this predicament was of his own doing. He was the one who had decided to pursue fame and fortune. No one had forced him.

He was tempted to slip into a childish pity party, but lying there, he remembered what the Apostle Paul had written to the church in Ephesus:

> In Christ we have redemption through his blood, the forgiveness of our trespasses, according to the riches of his grace that he lavished on us. (Eph 1:7–8)

God's grace was lavish! The knowledge of a God who is willing to forgive filled Caleb with peace and hope. Caleb asked for forgiveness for messing things up and asked God to straighten things out. This line of thinking caused Caleb to recall something else that the Apostle Paul had written to the church in Ephesus:

> For we are what God has made us, created in Christ Jesus for good works, which God prepared beforehand to be our way of life. (Eph 2:10)

God had known that Caleb would make this misstep from the beginning of time. However, God, being who God was, still had plans for Caleb to do good works in this world.

After some time, Doc called to Caleb from the porch and invited him to come along as he went to visit some familiar congregants. One after another, the people he visited told him how much they missed him. Everyone had a story of one or another of his athletes who was either doing great or in need of help. The latter, the stories of kids who needed him, were heart wrenching. These stories made him long to come home for good. Wouldn't it be true that if this were where God wanted to use him, then the money would be enough?

No sooner had he convinced himself to come home than the thought occurred to him that he could not just quit his job. It was too drastic a measure. Nothing catastrophic had happened at Grandville. He had been able to navigate the landmines pretty well by staying to himself. His problems were small potatoes. Maybe he was supposed to be an example to the wealthy kids at Grandville. Besides, quitting and going home would look too much like failure. He would stay and make something respectable out of it.

＊＊＊

Back in his Washington, DC office, Caleb reached over his head toward the credenza behind him, and picked up a baseball he kept there. "Ask away," he cheerfully demanded of me.

"Okay!" I complied, "You were painfully waffling back and forth. Why?"

"Oppressors don't usually attack in big ways—they are subtle. We'd react to—maybe even fix—something big. The oppressor wants to keep it subtle so you don't notice until it is too late—like 'a little fox that ruins the vineyards.'[5] Oppressors tempt us with the seemingly insignificant things that only become big after we are hooked. A little fox is a bargain on a five-dollar t-shirt that seems like an innocent enough purchase until you learn a child sat sewing in a sweatshop instead of going to school all so you could dress cheaply. A little fox is a forty-cent tomato picked by someone working ten-hour days and being paid less than a living wage so you could have a

---

5. Song 2:15.

fast food burger with a slice of tomato on top. We commonly don't realize the little fox is ruining the whole vineyard until it is too late."[6]

"So it is with spiritual warfare," continued Caleb. "It is the seemingly insignificant, 'not so bad' things that will catch up with you. A little fox might be gossip, selfishness, or pride.[7] In reality, these things aren't 'little' at all. They are highly destructive. Yet, somehow, we think of them as small. My desire for a better paying job in lieu of my true calling was a little fox. It doesn't even seem wrong from a worldly perspective. Yet, it wasn't what God had created me to do. So there I was lured to Rufus's harem, but now refusing to get in bed with him. All the while, the Shepherd is right there calling me to come away. Like the Shulammite, I want to go. I even say to God, 'You are mine and I am yours.' However, when it comes right down to it, she and I both send the Shepherd away instead of accepting his invitation."

Reggie wondered if I recognized the Shulammite's words, "You are mine and I am yours."[8] They were the words of the ancient covenant agreement between God and Abraham.[9] I had not recognized them, but after some research, I came to understand how significant these words were. We usually hear the covenant agreement from God's perspective, "I will be your God, and you shall be my people," but here the Shulammite speaks the words of the covenant to the Shepherd. This is no accident. It demonstrated her desire to seal her love for the Shepherd in a covenant promise—permanent and unbreakable.[10] However, even though her desire was to make this commitment and, in fact, she thought that she *had* made this commitment, she immediately failed by sending her Shepherd away and refusing his invitation to come away with him. It had been the same with Abraham. He may have desired to uphold his side of the agreement, but being human, it was never a real possibility.

However, God was under no misunderstanding. God had always known that humanity would fail at being God's people. It was a given. Yet,

---

6. Malaty, *A Patristic Commentary*, 62. The second-century scholar, Origen, when writing about "little foxes" emphasized the word "little" saying that "as long as an evil thought is still immature, it can easily be cast out of the heart." However, if it is allowed to stay for a while and grow, "it brings the soul to a point of consent" which is sin.

7. Glickman, *A Song for Lovers*, 49–50.

8. Song 2:16.

9. Gen 17:7–8, Exod 6:7, and Lev 26:12. God exchanged these vows with Abraham on behalf of humanity. His family, as the chosen people, was to invite the rest of the world to take part in God's covenant.

10. Pope, *Song of Songs*, 405.

God had decided to keep God's part of the covenant even though humanity could not. It was the same with the Shulammite. She would make this commitment now, then again toward the end of the Song.[11] And yet, the Shepherd knew that she would waffle back and forth in her determination to follow him. But the Shepherd would never break his side of the covenant. His love was not dependent on how good she was at loving him back or how quickly she would come away with him. The Shepherd would always love the Shulammite, even when she sent him away.

Caleb summarized his answer to my original question, "I too loved the Good Shepherd, but I kept going back and forth fighting my selfish desires. Fortunately, the Good Shepherd didn't give up on me either."

"Caleb, will you please say more about the Good Shepherd showing up at her window? Does this illustrate that God is only with us every now and then?"

"In reality, God is always there even when the evidence says otherwise." Caleb quoted one of his favorite verses:

> Although you have not seen him, you love him; and even though you do not see him now, you believe in him and rejoice with an indescribable and glorious joy. (1 Pet 1:8)

There were more verses in Scripture like this. Reggie quoted the author of Hebrews who claims God "will never leave you or forsake you."[12]

Pulling this all together, I could see that when the Shulammite opens her eyes to the hills surrounding her, then the Shepherd comes, leaping and bounding to gaze at her. It shows how the Shepherd, her Beloved, can't wait to be with her even though she was the one who got herself into this mess.[13] He wants her to see him and welcome him. It is a beautiful illustration of how much God loves us and of the delight God takes in us.[14]

To Caleb, I summarized, "God 'showed up' in your life because you made space for God in that hammock."

"Yes." Caleb went on as if he were carefully choosing each word, thinking it through as he talked. "We are meant to make intentional space for God—to engage in deep listening prayer. That said, the truth is that I hadn't been intentional about it that day. God reached out to me. God took the

---

11. Song 6:3.
12. Heb 13:5.
13. Exum, *Song of Songs*, 125–26.
14. Assis, *Flashes of Fire*, 80.

opportunity of my being alone and in a place where I felt safe to speak to me. Never underestimate the power of God's love to reach out to us. God can create a place to be alone with us even in "the midst of our enemies." Do you know that reference?"

Reggie knew, "Psalm 23. 'The Lord is my Shepherd.'"

"Amen to that!" responded Caleb as he leaned forward in his chair. "God not only seeks us first and relentlessly, but God sets the table for us even when we are surrounded by unjust systems that want to consume us.[15] Since that time in my life, I have learned to intentionally create space to listen to God. This is the most important thing a follower of Christ can do. How else can you be close to God and get God's guidance for your life? In fact, the Shepherd tells the Shulammite, 'let me see your face, let me hear your voice.'[16] She has looked for the Shepherd too infrequently.[17] The Good Shepherd wants us to set aside time to gaze at him and to speak to him. Sure I had prayed every now and then when I was especially overwhelmed, but I hadn't spent enough alone time with God just listening."

"Why doesn't the Shulammite go with the Shepherd? The way he calls her to himself is beautiful with birds singing, the earth coming to life. She even professes her love for him. Why doesn't she follow him? What is stopping her?"

"She thinks that she can't!" exclaimed Reggie. "She sees a garden wall between them. Just like the prophet Isaiah, who told humanity that their sin had built a wall between themselves and God, the Shulammite is letting sin—unjust systems and the oppressor—hold her back from following the Shepherd.[18] In actuality though, that wall can't contain her spirit."

Reggie's assessment of the Shulammite was right. It was the same reason that had caused Caleb to stay where he was too. Caleb had no savings from all the years at Harrelson. What little he had had was spent on doctors during his wife's illness. He needed a job to feed, house, and clothe himself. Therefore, like the Shulammite, he says to his Shepherd, "Until the day breathes and the shadows flee, turn, my beloved, be like a gazelle or a young stag on the cleft mountains."[19] In other words, "I love you, yet it is not safe for us to be together. I have no choice but to send you away, but please stay

---

15. Soughers, *Falling in Love with God,* 53.

16. Song 2:14.

17. Glickman, *A Song for Lovers,* 48.

18. Isa 30:13 and 59:2.

19. Song 2:17.

where I can see you from time to time." Neither the Shulammite nor Caleb thought that they could escape from the harem. Therefore, for the time being, they had both decided to play along with the system until it would let go of them on its own.

Caleb added, "What we both needed to understand was that unjust systems do not dismantle themselves. Unjust systems must be dismantled. The Good Shepherd doesn't need the unjust system to let go before he can scoop us up and carry us away. In addition, no matter what the situation, nothing can separate us from God. We must understand these things so that we are free to dismantle injustice. Otherwise, we will always be captive waiting unsuccessfully for the unjust system and the oppressor to go away on their own. And that isn't going to happen."

"Caleb, it still seems to me that there is a bit of a difference between you and the Shulammite. I keep coming back to the fact that she was physically imprisoned. It may be a luxurious trap, but she can't just walk away. You could have."

Caleb patiently explained again—this time from a slightly different angle. "Unjust systems can control our bodies, but they can't control our spirits if we refuse to participate in them. And to stop participating, all we have to do is say "yes" to the Good Shepherd. When we do that a whole new world opens up to us like spring bursting forth—like a table set in the presence of our enemies. It is, in a sense, our resurrection."

"So by saying yes to the Shepherd, she might still be trapped physically, but freed spiritually by refusing to play the harem's game."

"Exactly! Many African-American slaves were in this situation before the Civil War. Their bodies were bound to the master. They could not walk away. But their hearts were bound to God. Saying yes to the Shepherd transcends the physical world. It changes everything—breathes life and purpose into one's soul and gives self-respect that didn't exist before. A person who says yes to the Good Shepherd lives to serve God and not the oppressor. This is the peaceful resistance that MLK Jr. taught where one resists the oppressor by saying yes to the ways of God—yes to loving, forgiving, and even serving the enemy. MLK Jr. stopped playing into the unjust system when he started teaching the oppressed to love the oppressor. Unjust systems only work when you fear or hate the oppressor. When you love the oppressor, the system can be dismantled. Saying yes to the Shepherd is the first step."

The Shulammite Regrets Sending the Shepherd Away

Song 3:1–5

SETTING:	The HAREM's bedroom inside KING SOLOMON's country estate.
AT RISE:	It is now nighttime. The SHULAMMITE is waking from sleep.

SHULAMMITE

[3:1] Upon my bed at night I sought him whom my soul loves; I sought him, but found him not; I called him, but he gave no answer.[1] [3:2] "I will rise now and go about the city, in the streets and in the squares; I will seek him whom my soul loves." I sought him, but found him not. [3:3] The sentinels found me, as they went about in the city. "Have you seen him whom my soul loves?"

---

1. The Shulammite sleeps restlessly, worrying over having sent her Shepherd away.

[3:4] Scarcely had I passed them, when I found him whom my soul loves. I held him, and would not let him go until I brought him into my mother's house, and into the chamber of her that conceived me.[2,3]

> (Happy that she has found her SHEPHERD again, the SHULAMMITE once again turns to the HAREM and encourages the women to resist their situation.)

[3:5] I adjure you, O daughters of Jerusalem, by the gazelles or the wild does: do not stir up or awaken love until it is ready!

✳ ✳ ✳

Back at Rufus's lodge, as the sun started to go down, Caleb moved from the hammock to a lounge chair that was sitting on the deck attached to the boathouse. From there he had a view of the sun setting into the lake. The display of colors spanning the sky was amazing, as was the reflection of the colors in the lake. As soon as the sun was down and the fireflies came out, he realized that he could get used to living like this—a grand house, a lake of his own, surrounded by nature. Why shouldn't he live like this too?

It was then he heard her voice, "Howdy stranger!" It was Hallie. She was dressed in distressed jeans rolled up to show her ankles and a white button-down shirt with most of the buttons unbuttoned exposing a lace camisole. She pulled a lounge chair up next to his, kicked off her sandals, sat down, and smiled.

He immediately sat up. Caleb was speechless. As he looked toward her, he could see the lodge brightly lit up behind her. He immediately went from feeling restful to feeling an overwhelming dread. He was in no mood to deal with the entire Bennett clan tonight. He didn't know what Rufus was up to, but obviously, he had something up his sleeve. Most likely Rufus wanted him to do something that he otherwise wouldn't have done like look the other way while the team was pumped full of drugs before the game.

2. Harper, *The Song of Solomon*, 21. "Into my mother's house, into the chamber of her that conceived me," signifies that she won't be satisfied until she has made a public commitment to the Shepherd.

3. Godet, "The Interpretation of the Song of Songs," in Kaiser, *Classical Evangelical Essays in Old Testament Interpretation*, 163. Godet points out the contrast between the first chapter of the Song, where the King brings the enslaved Shulammite into his chambers, and this chapter of the Song, where she dreams of being a free woman who brings the Shepherd in to her mother's chambers.

Any sense that God was near had vanished again. Why did God suddenly seem so absent? Was this being cast back and forth between peace and emptiness going to last forever?

Hallie, on the other hand, seemed unusually relaxed. She pointed to a star formation in the sky, "That is Scorpio." It wasn't Scorpio. It was Orion's Belt.

"Nice try Hallie. But . . ." They lay in their loungers side by side as Caleb walked her through the stars and the African stories that he had learned as a child that went with the different formations.

"When did you get here?" asked Hallie

"Early this afternoon."

"Did you get any rest?" Hallie had always been nice to Caleb, but right then she seemed genuinely interested in him as a person. He had had no one to talk to in Grandville for so long. Why not ask Hallie what she thought? Plus staying out here and talking to Hallie was far more desirable than being confronted by the rest of the Bennetts. The longer he could delay that the better. Perhaps Hallie had a spiritual side.

"I had an encounter with God today."

"Really?" she asked making sure that he was serious. Convinced he was, she asked him to tell her about it.

So he told her about his experience that afternoon. He shared his deepest thoughts with her about his guilt in leaving the kids at Harrelson. He told her that he had come to Grandville for the wrong reasons and now felt a boatload of guilt about that too. She was the first woman he had talked to about his innermost thoughts since his wife had died. It felt great.

When he was done, Hallie spoke up, "Can I give you some advice Caleb?"

"Yes, tell me what you know about finding God in the struggles of life?"

Hallie laughed. "Nothing! I sure as heck don't know anything about finding God, but I do know that Rufus is going to take care of you. I think you are just anxious because this is all so new. And I will let you in on a secret. Rufus has a big surprise for you this weekend."

"He does?" The dread in Caleb's voice was palpable. He looked back at the lodge again wondering what was going on.

"No—you are going to love it!" Hallie smiled and shook her head trying to convince him.

Caleb thought that over. "Tell me what it is?"

"No. But it is expensive and sexy."

"Sexy?"

"Yes. I am not saying anything else about it. But my advice is to stop worrying about God. Relax and enjoy the good stuff. Maybe you will find God in the good stuff. You found God here this afternoon and this place is definitely the good stuff—compliments of Rufus."

Looking at the stars reflected in the lake, Caleb asked out loud, "Is this really the good stuff?" They sat listening to crickets and bullfrogs without speaking until Caleb sat up to glance back at the lodge. Nodding toward it, he probed, "Surprised the rest of the gang hasn't made their way out here by now."

Hallie turned to look at what he was looking at—the house lights lit up both inside and out. "Oh, I'm alone. I had an alumni meeting at Wesleyan in Macon. I'm supposed to be on a girl's weekend away, but when Rufus mentioned you were already here, I started thinking about you—how lonely you must be here tonight all by yourself. So I drove on down. And from the sound of things, you needed someone to talk to."

"You're alone!" He wasn't containing his shock. "Every light in the lodge is turned on?"

"I turned them on looking for you." Her eyebrows lifted and she tilted her head slightly as she spoke. She was asking without using words if he was okay with her being there. Then she reached across to his chair, rested her hand on his wrist, and slowly ran her fingers back and forth across the veins in his arm.

Caleb's mind was going a hundred different directions. She was insane. There was no way this was going to turn out good. All people needed was the appearance of a married white woman having an affair with a black man and he would probably be lynched in both counties. Even if he did not participate in Hallie's plans, there would be hell to pay—everyone would assume they had been up to no good.

As if she read his mind, she said, "Don't worry. No one will ever find out." Hallie looked around like she was trying to find a way to erase the last five minutes and get back the feelings he had for her before he found out she was there alone. "Have you eaten?" asked Hallie.

"No," replied Caleb.

"Let's go into town and get something," suggested Hallie.

"You wanna go out to dinner with a black man? This is the Deep South. You crazy?"

"Let's go to a restaurant on your side of town. I've never been to a restaurant there before. And I guarantee you that I don't care what people think. They can think the worst if they want. Besides . . ." She wanted to make sure he was listening. Therefore, she emphasized what she would say next with a long breathy pause. When she was sure he was interested, her voice got involuntarily a bit deeper, "by the time we wake up tomorrow, I hope the worst is true."

He was tempted. She was the first woman to touch him in a long, long time and he craved for more. Then it dawned on him that everything he had just confided in her had floated into the night. Hallie hadn't understood or even listened. She had no concern for him or the things of God. She didn't care if he had purpose in his life or not. She was all about finding one more risky thing to do with her purposeless life—and the more risk, the sexier she felt. It was the only thing that kept her going. She didn't care about him or anything spiritual. Confiding in Hallie as if she might know something about God had been absurd.

He was asking the wrong person for advice. She would use him just like the rest of her family. She would hold whatever happened over his head and try to control him for the rest of his life. Hallie was damn attractive, but when he took time to think about her, she didn't appeal to him. He didn't like wild women. Frankly, their volatility scared him. He had married his wife for love and someday he intended to do that again.

Nevertheless, he couldn't figure out how to get out of this alive. If he rejected Hallie, she would make his life a living hell. Of that, he was sure. If he spent the night here, even in separate buildings, she would tell people that things had happened between them even if nothing did. The only thing he could do that might save him was to leave. Now!

He got up from the lounge chair letting her arm fall. "Hallie, I'm sorry you drove down here. Nothing is going to happen between us. I need to get my stuff and head over to my parents' house. I'll be staying there tonight."

"No!" begged Hallie.

"I'm sorry." Caleb got up and walked to the boathouse, collected his stuff, and went to his side of town. Rufus's lodge was in the county as opposed to being within the small city's limits. To get to his side of town, he drove past farms and undeveloped land for thirty minutes, then as he closed into town, he passed a few large homes on "the right side of the tracks" before crossing the railroad tracks where he ended up at Big Daddy's BBQ

House and sat down at the bar. Big Daddy was pleased to see him and gave him a bear sized hug.

After Caleb ordered, Big Daddy got on the phone and called a few of Caleb's buddies and eventually two men joined him. They were glad to see him. He was glad to see them too. There was no shortage of attention for Caleb as word got around town that he was there. Some of it even female attention. He spent several hours at Big Daddy's soaking it all up.

Eventually he knocked on his parents' door. He could see a yellow glow from his dad's office lamp. He knew his dad was still awake working on his sermon for Sunday so he could enjoy Caleb's scrimmage on Saturday. Caleb asked if he could spend the night. His dad had all sorts of questions about why he wasn't at Rufus's boathouse, but Caleb didn't answer them. To answer them with the truth meant admitting he had made a mistake leaving Harrelson. Answering with a lie meant lying to his dad. He wasn't going to do either. Therefore, he simply didn't answer.

Doc Morgan knew better than to question him further. So he let it go.

✱✱✱

Instead of our regular meeting place and time, Caleb had taken Reggie and me to Sunday brunch in Georgetown near where I lived. As usual, when the story started to wind down, I asked Caleb some questions.

"Caleb, relate the evening you just told me about to the Shulammite."

"It was in the quiet of my old bedroom in my parents' house that night where I first realized I was the Shulammite."

"Explain!"

"Coming home to my parents' house because I had nowhere else to stay at fifty-four years of age was a humbling experience. My dad was working on his sermon. Whenever Doc had the opportunity, between the time he would finish his research and start organizing his thoughts, he liked to have someone to bounce ideas off of. That night, I had come home at just the right time. Guess what he was preaching on?"

"The Song of Solomon?"

"You got it! He had been preaching a series. As I was soon to find out, her story was my story. In her dreams, the Shulammite begins to regret sending her Shepherd away and she wants him back, but he is no longer standing at the harem's window."

Caleb put down his fork and looked at me to make sure I was following him. "I was still trying to make things work my way—to salvage the decision to come to Grandville. I was calling God, 'my Beloved,' instead of following God over the walls of Grandville into the freedom that awaited. I too had sent God away. And when you do that, the unjust system tries tightening its grip around you."

"Hence Hallie showing up?"

"It jolted me that night to think I was tempted to fall into her trap. I didn't really like her, but it felt so great to be desired that I could have easily said yes. Similarly, the Shulammite, regretting that she had sent her Shepherd away, runs into the marketplace looking for him and asks the first people she sees, the sentinels, for help."

"You asked Hallie for help."

"Just as stupid as asking the sentinels. The Shulammite was a concubine and the sentinels were there to protect the king's interests—not to help her find her Shepherd. I don't think they knew who she was at that point. Nevertheless, they will remember her. And she has stupidly showed her hand to them risking everything. When they realize who she is, they will know that her loyalties are not with the King, but with her Shepherd."

I posed something else to Caleb, "In the Song it says that the Shulammite had 'no sooner' passed them by than she found her Shepherd. Is that significant?"

"I think it is. After she stops asking the wrong people for help, she is able to find her Shepherd."

"And likewise with you and Hallie. You pass her by—you tell her no—and it is like a rite of passage for you."

"Yes. When saying yes to God is hard, then we often to try to find God in places or people where God isn't there.[4] I was fortunate that it didn't take long to find God again at my parents' house through the preview of Doc's sermon that night. But seeking God is not just one event. It is a lifetime journey for the follower of Christ."

The waiter came by to check on us, interrupting Caleb's flow. As soon as he left, Caleb picked right back up, "There will be times when we feel God has gone missing, but nothing will make us feel more like God is missing than when we are caught up in an unjust system that cares nothing about us—where the truth is being mocked and trampled on. To begin dismantling injustice, we must sit down at the table God has prepared for

4. Soughers, *Falling in Love with God*, 61.

us in the presence of our enemies. This is the same as saying yes to God. It is then that the unjust system will lose control over our souls. That is when we are ready to serve God and God alone."

Reggie interjected, "What strikes me is how many ways we can seek God in the wrong places without ever being aware that that is what we are doing. We can ask directions from the person who knows nothing or doesn't have our best interests in mind. We can look for God in sex—that was what Hallie was doing even though she didn't realize it. We accept 'truths' that are part lies like the truth that money can make us happy. Then we start participating in the unjust system and it will devour us."

Smiling, I blurted, "Reminds me of that song 'Looking for Love in all the Wrong Places.'" Both men looked at me as if I were crazy. I sang the first line. Still no hint of recognition in their eyes. "Johnny Lee?" I asked suspiciously.

"Who?" said Reggie looking over at Caleb. Caleb shrugged his shoulders.

"You've never heard the song? Really?"

"You are talking to two black men. Got anything by Marvin Gaye?" laughed Reggie as he elbowed Caleb. Then they both laughed at me.

We had closed down the brunch crowd and were alone in the restaurant. I stood gathering my papers and tape recorder into my messenger bag. "As a matter of fact, I do have some Marvin, but it is for Hallie." I snapped my fingers, swayed a bit, and started singing "Let's Get It On." Reggie joined in. Caleb hummed in the background before he raised his water glass and said, "To Hallie!"

"To Hallie!" Reggie and I clinked glasses with Caleb.

Reggie and I walked Caleb to his car. After a short goodbye, in which I couldn't resist hugging Caleb, he drove off and left the two of us standing in the parking lot alone. It had been three weeks since Reggie and I had spent the afternoon getting coffee and exploring the museum together. On one hand, I was disappointed that he hadn't shown any interest in spending more time with me. On the other hand, we were both in demanding jobs that took up all of our time. Maybe he was interested and just busy. I summoned all the courage I had and asked him if he had to go right away or if he could walk me home.

"I'm sorry. I have to catch up on some work before Monday." Immediately, I could tell from the look on his face that I had crossed a line. My heart skipped a beat. Maybe two.

I knew Reggie well enough that he had not turned me down because he thought it was out of line for a woman to ask him to go for a walk with her. The only thing I could assume was that he just wasn't interested in me. I could also tell it hurt him to turn me down. He was such a kind man that he didn't want to hurt my feelings, which made me like him all the more.

Feeling rejected, I put on a good face, wished him well on the work he had to get done, and headed home.

SPIRITUAL PRACTICE 5

Praying the Labyrinth

Several things happened in verses 2:10–15 of the Song that reflect the Shulammite's journey toward a deeper relationship with God where unjust systems and the oppressor have no spiritual power:

- The Good Shepherd invited the Shulammite to come away with him. He even told her about what their relationship would be like free of the unjust systems in which she had been caught.

- The Shulammite thought she was onboard. She expressed her love for the Shepherd, but did not realize that she was holding back. She didn't trust the Shepherd's ability to protect her from the unjust system. Instead of following him, she sent the Shepherd away under the misguided notion that she was protecting him.

- The Good Shepherd appeared before the Shulammite again. The more they were together, the more he was able to teach her. He warned her against distractions (little foxes) that would told her back from the wholeness he desired for her.

As we pray the labyrinth, we will reconstruct this journey and let it speak into our own lives.

How to Pray the Labyrinth

If you have access to a real labyrinth, I encourage you to use it some of the days you practice this discipline—if not all of the days. If you do not

122

have access to a real labyrinth, there are many finger labyrinths available on the internet.[1] You may find it helpful to make copies and then use colored pencils or markers to color your way through it each day. Before you enter the labyrinth, hear God speaking to you in Song 2:10: "Arise, my love, my fair one, and come away." Pause and meditate on God's invitation. Begin your journey through the labyrinth. Stop every few steps and read a phrase from Song 2:11–13a printed below. Use these verses to bask in the love that God feels for you and meditate on the relationship that God wants with you:

- The winter is past, the rain is over and gone.
- The flowers appear on the earth;
- The time of singing has come,
- And the voice of the turtledove is heard in our land.
- The fig tree puts forth its figs,
- And the vines are in blossom; they give forth fragrance.

When you arrive at the center of the labyrinth, read:

> Arise, my love, my fair one, and come away. O my dove, in the clefts of the rock, in the covert of the cliff, let me see your face, let me hear your voice; for your voice is sweet, and your face is lovely. (Song 2:13b–14)

If you are ready to make or renew a commitment to God, then show the Good Shepherd your face and speak to him. In other words, let God into your inner most thoughts and being.

When you are ready to walk out of the labyrinth, read the phrase from Song 2:15:

> Catch us the foxes, the little foxes that ruin the vineyards—for our vineyards are in blossom. (Song 2:15)

As you walk out, concentrate on the little distractions that keep you from following with the Good Shepherd. Ask what keeps you from walking with God fully in every area of your life.

---

1. The Labyrinth Society offers free downloads of finger labyrinths at https://labyrinthsociety.org/download-a-labyrinth.

Day 1–5

Follow the preceding instructions for Praying the Labyrinth. Afterwards, journal what God has revealed to you.

ACT 4

Love Triangle

"Very truly, I tell you, anyone who does not enter the sheepfold by the gate but climbs in by another way is a thief and a bandit. The one who enters by the gate is the shepherd of the sheep. The gatekeeper opens the gate for him, and the sheep hear his voice. He calls his own sheep by name and leads them out. When he has brought out all his own, he goes ahead of them, and the sheep follow him because they know his voice. They will not follow a stranger, but they will run from him because they do not know the voice of strangers."

—John 10:1–5

Solomon Seduces

Song 3:6—4:7

SETTING:	A balcony of KING SOLOMON's country estate.
AT RISE:	The SHULAMMITE, along with a few members of the HAREM, is standing on a balcony of the estate watching KING SOLOMON and his great entourage approaching in the distance.

SHULAMMITE

3:6 What is that coming up from the wilderness, like a column of smoke, perfumed with myrrh and frankincense, with all the fragrant powders of the merchant?

HAREM

3:7 Look, it is the litter of Solomon![1] Around it are sixty mighty men of the mighty men of Israel, 3:8 all equipped with swords and expert in war, each with his sword at his thigh because of alarms by night. 3:9 King Solomon made himself a palanquin from the wood of Lebanon.[2,3] 3:10 He

---

1. A litter is a traveling couch.

2. Horine, *Interpretive Images in the Song of Songs,* 112. A palanquin was Solomon's throne or throne platform—a place where justice was dispensed.

3. Harper, *The Song of Solomon,* xviii. Lebanon is mentioned eight times in the Song.

made its posts of silver, its back of gold, its seat of purple; its interior was inlaid with love.

EUNUCHS

(The EUNUCHS call to the HAREM to join them at the entrance of the estate where they are to greet KING SOLOMON.)

Daughters of Jerusalem, ^{3:11} come out. Look, O daughters of Zion, at King Solomon, at the crown with which his mother crowned him on the day of his wedding, on the day of the gladness of his heart.[4]

KING SOLOMON

(KING SOLOMON reaches his country estate. Upon seeing the SHULAMMITE, he goes over to talk to her, ignoring the rest of the HAREM.)

^{4:1} How beautiful you are, my love, how very beautiful! Your eyes are doves behind your veil. Your hair is like a flock of goats, moving down the slopes of Gilead. ^{4:2} Your teeth are like a flock of shorn ewes that have come up from the washing, all of which bear twins, and not one among them is bereaved.[5] ^{4:3} Your lips are like a crimson thread, and your mouth is lovely. Your cheeks are like halves of a pomegranate behind your veil. ^{4:4} Your neck is like the tower of David, built in courses; on it hang a thousand bucklers, all of them shields of warriors.[6] ^{4:5} Your two breasts are like two fawns, twins of a gazelle, that feed among the lilies. ^{4:6} Until the day breathes and the shadows flee, I will hasten to the mountain of myrrh and

---

Harper believes that King Solomon's country estate was in or near Lebanon. However, Lebanon is usually considered just north of Solomon's Northern Kingdom.

4. Exum, *Song of Songs*, 150–51. Exum suggests that the crown was not a crown of kingship, but a wedding tradition that had nothing to do with becoming the monarch. Solomon's mother was Bathsheba. The story of Solomon's coronation is in 1 Kgs 1. It does not happen on his wedding day. Furthermore, a concubine would not have had a wedding, so he is not wearing it in preparation to wed the Shulammite. He is already "married" many times over.

5. Smith, "Song of Solomon: The Defeated King," disc 3. King Solomon is praising the Shulammite for having all of her teeth and that they are clean.

6. Ibid., Disc 3. In Eastern culture, the neck spoke of one's personality. A "bent neck" meant the person was shameful. The description of the Shulammite's neck, a strong tower, shows that Solomon thought she had strong character.

the hill of frankincense. **4:7 You are altogether beautiful, my love; there is no flaw in you.**

(The SHULAMMITE pays him no attention and the scene ends.)

∗∗∗

Caleb woke in his boyhood home to the smell of buttermilk biscuits and country ham frying in a skillet. His mother had always been the ultimate Southern cook. He was to enjoy an early breakfast with his parents before heading back over to Rufus's ranch to retrieve his sunglasses from the patio table. His parents voiced their disappointment that the black players from Harrelson weren't allowed to use the locker rooms at Williamson High, the white high school where the game was being played.

His dad affectionately mocked Caleb, "Boy, I thought you were going to get all this discrimination and racism straightened out? What gives?"

Caleb smirked at his dad. Then he realized what his parents were telling him, "You mean to tell me that Harrelson isn't going to be allowed in the locker room at Williamson? Only the white boys from Grandville?"

Doc raised his eyebrows and shook his head yes, "So you weren't aware?"

Caleb's mother chimed in, "Caleb, what do you think that says to our boys? Their ex-coach." She emphasized *ex* as she poked him with her finger, "Their ex-coach is prancing through the white boys' school while they aren't even allowed in the building?"

"I had no idea."

"Well, it's too late to do anything about it. Put it out of your head and eat your food."

Caleb ate as he was told, soaked up the good vibes that still lingered in the air despite that disturbing news, and left for Rufus's lodge.

Caleb didn't intend to go in. He was just going to retrieve the sunglasses from the table at the boathouse and head on over to the field where his team would be arriving for practice.

When Caleb arrived at the lodge, Jake was pulling into the long tree-lined driveway ahead of him. Jake's son and few of his friends, who were also teammates, were with him. The boys went straight to the boathouse and readied some fishing rods hoping for a quick catch. Jake, smiling, held up a bag of donuts in an offer to share them with Caleb.

"No thanks."

"You've been out already this morning? I expected to find you sleeping in." Pointing at Hallie's car in the turnaround, he added, "I see Hallie made it down from her board meeting this morning."

"Jake, she came up last night." Caleb waited to see Jake's reaction. There wasn't much of one. He just did what Jake usually did. He hung his head and wagged it back and forth.

"I spent the night at my parents' house."

Jake breathed in deep and dropped his head even lower. He had no words.

Caleb knew it was time to say something, "Jake, it's none of my business, but the two of you are playing with fire."

"I can't control her, Caleb. She does whatever she wants. She doesn't care about the rules."

"Jake, it isn't just her who isn't playing by the rules. I know about your escapades too."

Again, Jake didn't look surprised. His head still hung low, but Caleb couldn't tell what he was thinking. Was Jake remorseful or was this just an act?

"It's all true. But there is nothing to be done about it. There's no love in this marriage. Hallie grew up on the wrong side of the tracks. Her daddy left her when she was a kid. She was raped in high school by a senior classman before I even knew her. When I met her, I was a quiet athlete who had never been around girls much. I was shy and bored with life. She was the hottest, most exciting girl I'd ever laid eyes on. As it would turn out, she never felt the same way about me. She was just after my family's money and status. We got married and Daddy paid her way to college."

"If you want my advice," Caleb waited, hoping to be asked. Jake looked up at him. He didn't say no and he didn't say yes, so Caleb went on. "First you need to get yourself in line. Break it off with the redhead. Then you need to get Hallie some help. Maybe the two of you could go to counseling together. But trying to solve your problems by playing around with other people's hearts isn't right Jake. It hurts you, them, and your entire family."

Jake looked directly into Caleb's eyes. Caleb could tell that Jake wanted to be better than this. There was such deep hurt inside Jake. He turned away and covered his eyes and forehead with his right hand. Tears flowed down his face. He mumbled, "I can't do anything right. I never could."

"Now Jake, I'm going to sound like the preacher's son that I am. But there is one thing Doc taught me and that is you don't have to work to please God. You just have to accept God's love. I think if you start with accepting God's love and stop trying to find someone else to love you, then you'll find being the man you want to be comes naturally—loving Hallie will come naturally too. But if you keep chasing love where there is only lust, you're going to find you've got nothing left of your soul in the end. And you're going to hurt a lot of other people in the process."

* * *

Caleb broke out of storytelling mode and spoke candidly to me, "That morning, I honestly thought Jake might do an about face and become the man that he was meant to become. Hallie needed him to. Their son needed him to. The whole town needed him to."

"What happened to Jake?"

"He didn't stand strong for his marriage any more than he had for ending his son's drug use. It would have required that he break free from an unjust system that he had been part of all of his life. The system that kept him and his family tied to his father's purse strings. The system that made him look for love in sex with women he could only use and hurt. He wasn't willing to give any of it up. Partly because he believed what the system had told him all his life—that he was worth nothing outside of Grandville. And partly because it was just too painful to take a stand."

* * *

The Grandville bus arrived at the field about lunchtime. Surprisingly, every boy on the team showed up. Hallie brought her boys and their friends over from Rufus's lodge. Standing outside the field and leaning on the fence, she was able to get within a few feet of Caleb. Not willing to give up, and even though his back was facing her, she took advantage of the fact that he was alone. She commenced telling him in graphic detail what he had missed by *not* spending the night with her. Caleb's only response was, "Is that so." He walked onto the field with his back still to her, leaving Hallie to talk to herself.

Realizing he could no longer hear her, she shouted, "Rufus is going to be arriving at noon. He wants a word with you and the team when he gets here."

With the same level of sarcasm as before, Caleb repeated, "Is that so."

"He has a gift for you. Better not disappoint him."

Caleb didn't respond to Hallie. Practice went well. Doc and his mom had shown up to watch. He had forgotten that Rufus was on his way until practice had broken for the lunch that the Pep Club had set up in the parking lot. Out of the corner of his eye, he saw something happening. Players were creating an opening for a car that was driving slowly straight up through the lunch crowd. As it got closer and the crowd thinned to the right and left, Caleb could see Rufus driving a convertible. Behind him was Wade driving Rufus's Daimler Sovereign—a car Rufus only took out of the garage for special occasions. It was quite decadent. Rufus's convertible turned out to be a brand new 1968 blue Chevrolet Corvair convertible—a two-door, blue interior, four-speed manual stick shift beauty. Everyone was standing back, oohing over the car. What a car, indeed!

Rufus put the car in park, stepped out, and asked for everyone's attention, which he already had, of course. He proceeded to praise Caleb's hard work over the past five months. Then Rufus handed Caleb the keys to the convertible. Caleb's hand didn't move to receive them. He stood, expressionless, still staring at Rufus. Doc and his mom were standing immediately behind Rufus.

Rufus looked around at the crowd anxiously. "Son, it's yours. Come on now and take it for a spin." He nodded at the car with a look that insisted Caleb get in it immediately.

Still Caleb did not move. Instead, he said, "Rufus, I'd like for you to meet my parents."

"I see!" said Rufus turning to look at them. He reached around and shook Doc's hand, "Your son is a spectacular coach." Then turning his attention to Caleb's mother, took his baseball cap off and bowed a bit, "Good to meet you, ma'am."

Rufus was not going to let Caleb embarrass him. Smiling, he put his hand on Caleb's back and gave him a little push toward the car. In a voice that was forcing itself to stay calm, Rufus smiled and said, "Let's take the whole family for a ride!" As he spoke, he opened the passenger side door and ushered Doc and Caleb's mom into the back seat. By the look on Caleb's parents' faces, they were a little bit afraid of the man with the car. Not knowing what to do and not wanting to seem unfriendly, they got in. Rufus got in the front seat of the passenger's side. Still Caleb hadn't moved.

"Get in." Rufus said this time with a hint of anger peeking out around the edges.

Caleb got in. The crowd applauded. Hallie and Jake stood beside the driver's door clapping and saying things like "You deserve it!" and "Expecting great things from you!"

Caleb had done nothing to earn this car. He hadn't even been through a full season yet. It was simply a gift to impress and manipulate him. It was bad enough that he was being manipulated by Rufus, but Rufus had just expertly used his parents to get him into the car. For the first time, Caleb was mad.

Rufus must have sensed this, because on the drive around the school parking lot, he continued to praise Caleb's work and his parents' efforts in raising a fine son. Once around the parking lot and Caleb parked the car. The students ran over to look at it.

As Caleb helped his parents out of the car, Doc leaned over and said, "No pressure, but I would say that you better win tomorrow, son." The addition of "son" was in mimic of Rufus calling Caleb "son." Coming from Rufus, it wasn't exactly meant to be a putdown, but it was condescending to call a fifty-four year old man "son."

"What am I going to do, Dad? I can't accept this car. It isn't appropriate."

"No it isn't, but right now isn't the time to deal with it."

***

I broke into Caleb's story. "So Rufus planned this extravagant gift to be delivered on your own home turf so that he could show you the contrast between what he could offer you and where you came from. He wanted the choice to be clear between his riches and the poverty of your hometown."

"Absolutely. He was pulling out all the stops to get me to come to the dark side. Unjust systems often use the tactic of showing off their power and wealth to manipulate the foolish and greedy into hitching up their wagon to the oppressor's star."

I noted the obvious, "King Solomon was doing the same thing to the Shulammite. He sent her to his estate near her village and then made a big show of his arrival. He wanted her to have to weigh the cost of all he had to offer her compared to life in her little village."

"Yes, but God does the opposite of making a big show," chimed in Reggie. Reggie had been unusually quiet that morning. In fact, he hadn't been there when I arrived at Caleb's office. He snuck in after Caleb and I had already started without saying a word. That was bad enough, but it literally pulled at my heart when he didn't sit as usual in the other chair across from Caleb's desk. Instead, he sat on the couch on the other side of the room. The last thing I wanted to do was to lose Reggie's friendship so it seemed like a good idea just to let things get back to normal and give him whatever space he needed. I determined not to mention the coldness I suddenly felt from him.

Reggie was right about God doing the opposite of showing off power and wealth. God liked using the lowly instead of the powerful. For example, the Old Testament story that immediately came to my mind was when God sends Moses, a lowly shepherd, to the Pharaoh of Egypt to negotiate the release of the Hebrews.[7] Later, God sends David, also a lowly shepherd and still a child, to fight Goliath.[8] The Apostle Paul explains this phenomenon in the New Testament:

> Consider your own call, brothers and sisters: not many of you were wise by human standards, not many were powerful, not many were of noble birth. But God chose what is foolish in the world to shame the wise; God chose what is weak in the world to shame the strong; God chose what is low and despised in the world, things that are not, to reduce to nothing things that are, so that no one might boast in the presence of God. (1Co 1:26–29)

"God likes to show power through the powerless," declared Reggie thoughtfully. "No one should ever think that they are too small to be the one to confront the oppressor and dismantle injustice." That sounded cliché. Nevertheless, how many people are too intimidated to do anything except go along with whatever everyone else is doing?

"Before we take a break," Caleb glanced at his watch, "there is something that has stuck in my mind about the day Rufus gave me that car. Did you notice that Wade was driving Rufus's car?"

Reggie and I both shook our heads yes while shrugging in a way that said neither of us had thought much of it.

"Why did Rufus bring Wade with him? Wade had never been to a game before. Was Rufus afraid of being at the game with a black team? Was

7. Exod 3—11.

8. 1 Sam 17.

Rufus expecting trouble? Had Rufus planned trouble? Hallie and Jake were both there with their cars. Rufus didn't need his car to get back home. In fact, Hallie and Jake usually drove Rufus wherever he went. He wouldn't have been caught dead driving around town with Wade. Seems a little odd that Wade was there, don't you think?"

The Shepherd Romances

Song 4:8—5:1

SETTING: The HAREM's bedroom inside KING SOLOMON's country estate.

AT RISE: The SHULAMMITE is in the HAREM's bedroom. She peers out her window and there the SHEPHERD is again.

SHEPHERD

4:8 Come with me from Lebanon, my bride; come with me from Lebanon.[1] Depart from the peak of Amana, from the peak of Senir and Hermon, from the dens of lions, from the mountains of leopards.[2] 4:9 You have ravished my heart, my sister, my bride, you have ravished my heart with a glance of your eyes, with one jewel of your necklace.[3] 4:10 How sweet

---

1. The Shepherd calls her his "bride" which is in stark contrast to how the lustful Solomon sees her. Solomon sees her as the flavor of the week. Scripture speaks of the church as Christ's bride on many occasions. One example is Eph 5:31–32: "A man will leave his father and mother and be joined to his wife, and the two will become one flesh. This is a great mystery, and I am applying it to Christ and the church."

2. Harper, *The Song of Solomon*, 29. "Dens of lions and mountains of leopards" is a warning to the Shulammite that there is danger in staying with the King.

3. "You have ravished my heart" is literally translated as "You have un-hearted me" meaning she has stolen the Shepherd's heart. The lost sheep, the sinner, has stolen the heart of God. We are loved and adored by our Creator despite our missteps.

is your love, my sister, my bride! How much better is your love than wine, and the fragrance of your oils than any spice! [4:11] Your lips distill nectar, my bride; honey and milk are under your tongue; the scent of your garments is like the scent of Lebanon. [4:12] A garden locked is my sister, my bride, a garden locked, a fountain sealed. [4:13] Your channel is an orchard of pomegranates with all choicest fruits, henna with nard, [4:14] nard and saffron, calamus and cinnamon, with all trees of frankincense, myrrh and aloes, with all chief spices— [4:15] a garden fountain, a well of living water, and flowing streams from Lebanon.[4]

SHULAMMITE

[4:16] Awake, O north wind, and come, O south wind! Blow upon my garden that its fragrance may be wafted abroad. Let my beloved come to his garden, and eat its choicest fruits.

SHEPHERD

[5:1] I come to my garden, my sister, my bride; I gather my myrrh with my spice, I eat my honeycomb with my honey, I drink my wine with my milk.

HAREM

Eat, friends, drink, and be drunk with love.

***

After a short break, Caleb started by asking for my female take on all that I was learning about the Song.

"I am amazed at the great love the Shepherd has for her. I have read these verses over and over. Romance hasn't changed much in the last four thousand years! The Shepherd's words are beautiful. I also made a note to

---

4. Harper, *The Song of Solomon*, 32. "A garden fountain, a well of living water" can also be translated, "The fountain of my garden is a well of living waters." The Shepherd is saying that in his garden is a well of living water, which will flow through her. In John 7:37–38, Jesus cried out, "Let anyone who is thirsty come to me, and let the one who believes in me drink. As the Scripture has said, 'Out of the believer's heart shall flow rivers of living water.'"

myself to return to these verses if I am ever feeling far from God. If you believe that the Shepherd represents God, then to read the Shepherd's words and bask in them is a real treat for the soul!"

There was another thing that I had been pondering. It was the Shepherd's description of the Shulammite—her innermost being—as a garden locked and a fountain sealed. It seemed to contrast with how the Shepherd describes her just a verse later as a garden and a well of living water flowing from her. It doesn't take a big imagination to see the sensuality in these verses. Yet, the early church fathers saw Christ and his church. I wondered what Caleb's thoughts were on both the contrasting descriptions and the sensuality.

Caleb responded, "Metaphorically, I have always seen 'a garden locked' as a mystical place we invite God into—some would say it is our hearts. When God enters, out of us flows both the aroma of Christ—hence the fragrances that the Shulammite experiences—and his living waters."

Reggie pointed out that the Apostle Paul calls the followers of Christ "the aroma of Christ."[5] Likewise, the Gospel of John records Jesus saying, "The water that I will give will become in them a spring of water gushing up to eternal life."[6] In contrast, the Old Testament prophet Jeremiah wrote:

> My people have committed two evils: they have forsaken me,
> the fountain of living water, and dug out cisterns for themselves,
> cracked cisterns that can hold no water. (Jer 2:13)

The Shulammite is making a choice, to say yes to the Shepherd and let the fountain of living water flow through her or to say yes to the oppressor and become a cracked cistern. Caleb had the same choice before him.

Caleb remembered his feelings from that day, "You'd think a guy just given a brand new Chevy convertible would have been in hog heaven, but I was embarrassed that my parents had just gotten proof that they had been right and that I, a grown man, had made a decision based on greed. Who was I kidding? I wasn't doing anything for civil rights. Civil rights weren't about a black man becoming part of a white man's hell. Civil rights were about having the legal opportunity to serve God in the fullness of who God created us to be."

"So you didn't want to live in Rufus's harem?" I teased.

5. 2 Cor 2:15.
6. John 4:14.

"Oh what a deal that was! If I joined the harem, then I could have all my wishes come true. However, my soul would have rotted."

***

Back at Williamson High, as Caleb walked from the impromptu picnic area to the locker room, he passed his old beater car in the parking lot. He saw humor in the fact that he felt like the beater car looked hurt. He had bought that old car with his own money. It was already used, but he liked it. He didn't want Rufus's handout. Rufus was trying, as he had already done to Jake, to take Caleb's pride away—to make him believe that without Rufus, his life was lacking.

Inside the school building, where Caleb was allowed despite the color of his skin, he found a quiet hallway and sat there wondering what to do next. He hoped he would be alone for a few minutes. He was miserable and needed to think. Hallie, Rufus, and even his parents were pressuring him. Hallie and Rufus for selfish gain. His parents for good. But it was still pressure.

However, Caleb didn't get any time for himself. Next to the bench was a trashcan. Emanating from it was the smell of smoked fish. At first, it didn't register. Then he recognized the smell, not because he had smelled it before, but because he had read about it. Someone had been smoking amphetamines, which give off the smell of fish on the barbeque. The user had stupidly dumped the ashes in the trash. So on top of everything else he was feeling, Caleb was slapped in the face with what he already knew, but had pushed to the back of his mind. The team was still doing drugs. Just as he stood to look in the trashcan, his mother rounded the corner.

"Caleb, what are you doing going through the trash?" she laughed.

"I smelled drugs," he blurted out exhausted and beaten.

"You have a drug problem at Grandville?"

Caleb looked at her as if to say, "Give me a break, mom."

"Caleb, you don't need a shiny new car to be happy. Happiness and success is what happens inside you. You know this. At least you used to."

"I know mom." He found himself confessing to his mom, "I messed up by taking this job. Worst mistake in my life."

"Okay, but there isn't a mistake in this world that God can't use to teach us and make us stronger. You remember that too don't you?"

Without looking at his mother, he shook his head yes. "But I don't know what God wants me to do about it. Do I stay at Grandville and honor my contract or do I get myself fired because I won't let them pump these boys up with drugs? Or do I quit and become unemployed?"

"You are always welcome at our home until you find another job."

"Moving back in with my parents isn't as enticing as it might sound, mom."

Caleb's mom laughed again and patted her son on his back. Caleb turned and hugged her with one arm around her shoulders—the other still holding the top of the garbage pail. Then they both looked in the trashcan and took a whiff.

"Goodness gracious me!" declared his mom. "Is that what dope smells like?"

"Sort of," answered Caleb, putting the top back on the trashcan.

His mother sat down on the bench with her hand covering her nose. "Adopting you was the best thing we ever did. Your dad and I were deeply in love, but you gave our love a purpose as big as the universe. If I love you this much, imagine how God feels toward you. God loves you and created you for a purpose. But I declare to you that before you are going to be able to hear God's direction, you are going to have to see and feel how much God loves you and stop trying to pursue things—like fortune—that aren't the good God wants for you. You need to get your mind on God's love for you and let go of impressing anyone else—including me and your dad."

She was right and Caleb knew it. She was also preaching as if the gospel choir in Doc's church was going to burst into song any second.

"Mom, can I have a few moments alone?"

"If you show me where the women's room is."

"You know this is a white school. You know they don't want us in here."

"I do." She leaned up toward his face with her eyes wide and smiled, "Did you know segregation is over?"

"Only on paper."

"The restroom!" demanded his mom, "Point me toward it. There aren't any white women in the building right now anyway."

Caleb walked his mother to the bathroom and stood guard outside the door while he silently debated what to do with the evidence in the trashcan. He could report it to the police. He wondered if the police in South Georgia would care as much about protecting Rufus's grandson as they did back at

Grandville. Rufus would no doubt take any investigation as a declaration of war.

On the other hand, Caleb could keep it a private matter, stop the game, and send his team home as a disciplinary action. Rufus would like that only slightly more. Or he could do nothing, which is what Rufus would want him to do. What kind of human being would he be if he did nothing? He had a responsibility to these boys. Not only did amphetamines cause delusions, they impaired judgment. It had even been in the news lately that a world-class athlete had died of a heart attack after taking them.

His mom was right; he had to stop considering what would make himself look good, what would make others happy, and concentrate on God's love alone. God loved these boys and Rufus—what would God have Caleb do that expressed God's love to them? Then it dawned on him that the only evidence he had right then was a trashcan of ashes. But if they were getting high for practice, think of what they would be doing tomorrow for the game? They'd need to be caught in the act, if he was going to get those boys help.

After meeting with the team in the locker room, he talked the situation over with his dad who was friends with the local sheriff—a white man who had always been a friend of the black community. His dad used the school office phone to make an appointment with the sheriff. He was to meet them at Doc's house in forty-five minutes.

Caleb told the sheriff everything from the beginning. The sheriff listened without comment or interruption. When Caleb was done, the sheriff pointed out that athletic programs nationwide were seeing an increase in drug use. It was usually in affluent schools and as far as he was aware, the problem had not made it to South Georgia yet. "Oh it will make it down here soon enough," he was certain, "but these poor little Southern counties are always late adopters." There was no doubt in his mind that the boys from Grandville brought it with them.

The sheriff did not discuss his plan of action with Doc and Caleb, but promised them that if drugs were used at the high school on Saturday, the boys would be caught.

It was decided that Caleb should go back over to Rufus's lodge that night and spend the night in the boathouse as if nothing were amiss. After dark, Doc dropped Caleb off at the high school so he could pick up his new car and drive it to Rufus's. But as Caleb slid into the driver's seat of his shiny blue car, the unexpected feeling that he could get used to this luxury flowed over him. It was a very sweet ride. He put the roof down and savored it.

In fact, the ride was so sweet, that by the time he arrived at the lodge, Caleb was certain that there was no reason why he couldn't fix the drug problems, keep his new car, be a standout coach at Grandville, and finally stop living from hand to mouth. He put his bag in the boathouse and walked over to the pool where he sat on the diving board dipping his toes in the water. As he basked in the warm feelings that flowed over him, Hallie came out to the pool. "Would you like to join me in a midnight swim?" she asked.

"Hallie, about last night . . ."

"Have you changed your mind, Caleb?" she teased in that low voice she used when she wanted to sound sexy.

"No."

"You aren't staying at Grandville are you?"

"Maybe God wants me here."

"I knew you'd change your mind," she laughed.

"Hallie, I have no interest in pursuing a sexual relationship with you."

"I got that part, Caleb. I am talking about the car changing your mind. I think Rufus really did buy you with that car."

She stared at him and he stared back at her, but he wasn't actually looking at her. He was looking through her. He was angry that she—of all people—would question his motives. In fact, he was tired of everyone questioning his motives. Whatever happened to not judging others? He wanted to lash out at her, but he had no words.

"Enjoy it," she added as she removed Jake's shirt that was covering her yellow crocheted bikini and dove into the pool. "You've been bought like the rest of us," she taunted when she came up for air at the shallow end.

Her words hung in the air, but only as long as it took Rufus's grandson and two of his teammates to show up. Caleb watched them do cannon-balls into the pool. Watching Rufus's grandson, Caleb was reminded that the kid really didn't have what it took to be the kind of athlete that Rufus wanted Caleb to create. More than anything else, the kid didn't have the mental toughness. He was used to always getting his way. So when things on the field didn't go his way, he gave up rather than shake it off and try even harder. His physical skills were good, but nowhere near good enough. Caleb caught himself evaluating the boy as if he were Caleb's meal ticket with absolutely no interest in the boy's well-being. For an instant, Caleb no longer saw him as a child who should be protected from a grandparent who wanted to drug him, but as an obstacle who might stand in the way of Caleb's own personal success. Rufus would never keep Caleb around if his grandson failed to succeed.

***

Caleb ended our session there and summarized, "I wanted fancy things and they were calling my name. I even talked myself into believing that my relationship with God was good. Of course, I wasn't being completely honest. My commitment to God was incomplete. I was willing to do God's work on my terms—where I could get the things that I wanted. In truth, I was considering joining the unjust system."

"So you thought you could stay in the den of lions and do God's work? The Shepherd was calling the Shulammite to come away 'from the dens of lions, from the mountains of leopards!'"

"That brings up an interesting point," commented Caleb. "The Bible tells of many people who were called to serve God in the lion's den. They seem to do so with this kind of supernatural peace, joy, and love. They do it because God has sent them there—not so they can have a nice car. Moreover, they sure don't serve God by using another human being for their own profit. They want to serve the world, not benefit from its demise."

The rain was pouring down outside. The weatherman had gotten it wrong. He had predicted drizzle, not cats and dogs. One thing about Washington, DC was that the sky could grow darker in a storm than in any other city I had ever been in. As I stood and put my raincoat on, Caleb suggested I let Reggie drive me home. Reggie was standing behind Caleb putting documents on his desk that he had marked up to go over with Caleb. At Caleb's suggestion, Reggie glanced toward the wall behind me, but not at me. His expression showed that he was quite uncomfortable with the idea.

"Oh, I drove over this morning," I lied. "See you all next week!"

I walked down the stairs of the Cannon Office building and out a side exit so that there was no possibility they'd see me walking back to Georgetown.

Radical Prayer

Caleb is finding himself caught up in spiritual warfare. Part of him wants to do whatever God wants him to do and part of him wants a shiny new car and all the fringe benefits that go along with being in Rufus's harem. He finds himself turning the possibilities over and over again in his head trying to find a way to justify what he wants. When we are in similar situations, how do we know which direction God wants us to take? The Radical Prayer is one way to discover God's desires for us.

In the sixteenth century, Ignatius Loyola, the founder of the Society of Jesus (Jesuit Priests), wrote a prayer that offers everything we have to God. It is often called "The Radical Prayer." We will use it to ask God to put us in a frame of mind where we are open to doing anything that God calls us to do. The work of dismantling injustice is such that we have to be willing to follow Christ into the difficult places Christ goes. The Radical Prayer discipline should help us do that.

Things to keep in mind when you pray this prayer:

- God is love and God's direction will always be in the direction of love for all involved. It may be tough love, but it will always be love.

- Sometimes doing what God wants us to do (like building an ark on dry land) makes us look foolish to others.[1] Don't let looking foolish keep you from doing what God has called you to do.

1. Gen 5:32—10:1.

- The answer to your prayer may not come during your prayer time, or right away. Don't give up. Just do the discipline and be willing to wait for God's direction.

How to Pray the Radical Prayer

Days 1–5

First, pray the Radical Prayer slowly thinking over every word:

> Take Lord, and receive all my liberty, my memory, my understanding, and my entire will, all that I have and possess. Thou hast given all to me. To Thee, O lord, I return it. All is Thine, dispose of it wholly according to Thy will. Give me Thy love and Thy grace, for this is sufficient for me.

Second, tell God about the decisions or concerns that you are facing. Don't tell God what to do. Just lay out all of the options you can think of before God. Of course, God already knows the options. You are not laying them out to inform God, but to allow God to shine a holy light on your situation so that you will gain clarity for yourself.

Third, when you have explained the situation to God, stop talking to God and listen. Trust God to speak into your thoughts and in other ways in the coming days. Be open to hearing God however and whenever God chooses to talk to you.

Finally, journal what is revealed to you.

ACT 5

The Shulammite's Nightmare

In the time of King Herod, after Jesus was born in Bethlehem of Judea, wise men from the East came to Jerusalem, asking, "Where is the child who has been born king of the Jews? For we observed his star at its rising, and have come to pay him homage." When King Herod heard this, he was frightened, and all Jerusalem with him; and calling together all the chief priests and scribes of the people, he inquired of them where the Messiah was to be born. They told him, "In Bethlehem of Judea; for so it has been written by the prophet: 'And you, Bethlehem, in the land of Judah, are by no means least among the rulers of Judah; for from you shall come a ruler who is to shepherd my people Israel.'"

—Matthew 2:1–6

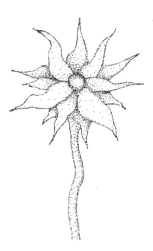

13

Beaten and Wounded

Song 5:2–8

SETTING: The HAREM's bedroom inside KING SOLOMON's country estate.

AT RISE: It is nighttime. The SHULAMMITE is returning to her room. It is obvious that she has been outside. She is bruised and dirty. Her coat is missing. She wakes the HAREM to tell them what has happened.

SHULAMMITE

[5:2] **I slept, but my heart was awake.**[1]

(The SHULAMMITE reenacts what has happened for the HAREM. She listens as if she can hear knocking.)

Listen! My beloved is knocking.

SHEPHERD

"Open to me, my sister, my love, my dove, my perfect one; for my head is wet with dew, my locks with the drops of the night."

1. Scholars debate over whether the Shulammite was asleep and is now telling the harem about a nightmare or if what she is telling the harem were actual events that she experienced. Either interpretation has the same outcome in the end—she deeply regrets turning the Shepherd away.

SHULAMMITE

(To the HAREM.)

5:3 I had put off my garment; how could I put it on again? I had bathed my feet; how could I soil them?

(The SHEPHERD reaches through the garden gate for the SHULAMMITE, begging her to open it.)

5:4 My beloved thrust his hand into the opening, and my inmost being yearned for him.

(The SHEPHERD withdraws his hand and disappears. The SHULAMMITE runs over to the garden gate and tries to unbolt the door, but her hands are slippery with the fancy cosmetics that she has put on her hands.)

5:5 I arose to open to my beloved, and my hands dripped with myrrh, my fingers with liquid myrrh, upon the handles of the bolt.

(She finally gets the gate open.)

5:6 I opened to my beloved, but my beloved had turned and was gone.

(She turns back to the HAREM again trying to justify herself.)

My soul failed me when he spoke. I sought him, but did not find him; I called him, but he gave no answer. 5:7 Making their rounds in the city the sentinels found me; they beat me, they wounded me, they took away my mantle, those sentinels of the walls.

(Turning to the HAREM.)

5:8 I adjure you, O daughters of Jerusalem, if you find my beloved, tell him this: I am faint with love.

***

As I left Caleb's office, the rain was coming down in torrents. The thunder and lightning seemed to be directly above my head. I couldn't walk all the way home in this weather. My choice was to return to the Cannon Office Building and wait it out or cross the street to the Library of Congress and hide out there for a while—except that was where I had run into Reggie before. He surely would think I was stalking him if he found me there again.

"Good grief!" I muttered under my breath. I tightened the cord of the hood on my raincoat, as if that would matter, and started walking down

Independence Avenue. It was a twenty-minute walk to the Air and Space Museum. By the time I reached it, it would be ten-fifteen, and the doors would be open to the public. I could wait out the storm there.

Halfway there, every inch of exposed skin and clothing was drenched. I felt completely stupid and rejected. My feelings were hurt. What on earth had I done that was so wrong? Why was Reggie treating me like this? I didn't want to go to the Air and Space Museum, I wanted to find a rock and crawl under it.

It was then that a car pulled up beside me. A familiar voice shouted, "Get in!" It was Reggie.

"I'm okay. I have an errand to run at the Air and Space Museum. But thank you anyway." I shouted over the thunder and started walking even faster.

Pulling up next to me again, he yelled, "Please! Get in."

"I'm almost there," I pointed toward the glass and gray block building still a distance down the street.

"I'm sorry. Please get in."

It was the "I'm sorry" that got me. I got in his car and Reggie drove me to my apartment in Georgetown without speaking a word other than asking for directions and an obligatory goodbye.

A week later, we met as usual in Caleb's office. I was determined to be friendly and Reggie seemed determined not to be cold to me. Caleb picked up where we had left off.

∗∗

The next day was the Grandville-Harrelson scrimmage. Except for a few lucky boys who got to stay at Rufus's lodge with his grandson, the team had spent the night at the local motor lodge. Caleb, on the other hand, awoke to a big breakfast prepared by a local who cooked for Rufus and his family whenever he was in town. Seeing the old black woman in a white servant's uniform standing in Rufus's kitchen turned Caleb's stomach. When she called Caleb "Sir," it was all he could take.

After breakfast, he decided to walk the estate. He began to pray about how he could help the people at Grandville. He asked God how he could make Rufus's grandson the star that Rufus wanted him to be. He asked God how he could influence Grandville for the good. How he could improve race relations. He prayed, having convinced himself that God wanted him to be their coach and enjoy the fancy things they offered him. He prayed passionately. Caleb talked to God for a long time. In fact, he never stopped talking to listen. He was in the spiritual struggle of his life. He was saying, "I love you God, but stay here with me inside this unjust system—ignore with me those who have been hurt by this system." Yet, if he had been still even for a moment, he would have heard God speak. God had not called him to Grandville.

The day started as planned. Soon the scrimmage began. It seemed that the entire student population of Grandville along with their families had shown up. The Grandville Baptist Church had brought two busloads of high schoolers. In addition, the whole black side of Harrelson turned out for the game. Even the Atlanta Constitution showed up to cover this first—a black team playing a (mostly) white team coached by a black coach. They promoted it as the game that proved segregation in the South was never the problem it had been trumped up to be. They failed to report that portable bathrooms had been brought in for the "colored folk." Nor did they report what was about to happen.

Caleb could see the sheriff and his wife in the stands. He was not in uniform, but tipped his baseball cap at Caleb. This reminded Caleb of all that was at stake that day. He hoped that the boys would be caught and the drug issue would be addressed once and for all. Then he would be free to do some real coaching at Grandville.

The game began. The two teams were evenly skilled. It looked like it was going to be a real contest to see who would win. Caleb was feeling far less stressed and much more relaxed as things got moving. But about thirty minutes into the game, a pillar of smoke appeared behind the stands on the left side of the pitcher's mound. Something was on fire in the parking lot. The game halted and someone made an announcement asking the crowd to stay in their seats. The firehouse had been called and a truck was on its way to put out a car that was on fire.

No sooner was the announcement over when an explosion rattled the stands. People started to panic. The gas tank of the car had exploded. Another announcement followed asking once again that everyone stay in their seats.

It was then that the sheriff found Caleb and motioned him into the dugout, "Your father and mother arrived late to the stadium and saw a man messing with your new car. Your father questioned what the man was doing and was attacked and beaten unconscious. Your mother was not hurt."

"Where are they?"

"En route to the hospital. Is there someone who can take over for you here? I think you need to go on to the hospital. One of my men will take you."

The next hour was a blur to Caleb. The officer driving him to the hospital told him that his mother was saying that the man who set the fire to Caleb's car was the same man who had driven his new car the day it was presented to him.

"Rufus set fire to my car?" asked Caleb in disbelief. "I doubt that. My mom must be confused."

"I don't think so—she was very calm," answered the officer. "Was there someone else in the car with Rufus?"

"Wade! Rufus's son-in-law," Caleb explained. "Now that makes sense. He was driving Rufus's car. He's a thug."

"Why would they give you a new car and then set fire to it?"

"Why would they give me a new car—period?"

After a few minutes of silence, the officer spoke hesitantly, "I want to say this cautiously, but I wonder if it's possible that Rufus had gotten word that we're going to be searching the locker room for drugs during the scrimmage?"

"Well, I sure haven't told anyone," answered Caleb.

"No, but maybe someone on the police force did? Rufus has long arms here in Georgia. And people have the idea that if they get a chance to do something for Rufus, he'll do something for them."

Caleb's father had been taken to the nearest hospital, which, thankfully, could no longer turn away African-Americans. When Caleb arrived at the hospital, he found his mother standing next to the emergency room bed where his father's comatose body lay. His father had sustained a serious injury to the head. Doc wasn't expected to live.

Grief overwhelmed Caleb.

During the next few days, an untold number of visitors came to the hospital leaving flowers and gifts at a makeshift reception area in the hospital lounge. If a man had ever been prayed over, it was Doc. He had been an icon in the community—the only black preacher—for more than sixty years.

Early the next morning before sunrise, a neighbor finally convinced Caleb's mom to go home for a while to get some food and sleep. The neighbor promised to bring her back later that morning.

It was then that Caleb was alone with his father for the first time. And it was then that Caleb confessed to his father what he had already confessed to his mother, "I was wrong to ever take this job. I did it because I was tired and greedy. I am no MLK Jr. struggling for civil rights. I am just selfish. All of this is my fault. Please forgive me, Dad."

It was as if Caleb couldn't quite get his mind set on the things of God until he saw evil full-faced. It was the same for the Shulammite. It wasn't until the city sentinels, King Solomon's warriors, caught her outside her quarters again looking for her Shepherd, that she was able to see the danger. This time the sentinels were ready for her. They beat her and took her coat.

Doc didn't react to Caleb's words.

Caleb reached for the Bible beside Doc's bed and began to read aloud the parable of the sower:

> Listen! A sower went out to sow. And as he sowed, some seeds fell on the path, and the birds came and ate them up. Other seeds fell on rocky ground, where they did not have much soil, and they sprang up quickly, since they had no depth of soil. But when the sun rose, they were scorched; and since they had no root, they withered away. Other seeds fell among thorns, and the thorns grew up and choked them. Other seeds fell on good soil and brought forth grain, some a hundredfold, some sixty, some thirty. Let anyone with ears listen! (Mat 13:3–9)

In other words, some seeds fell into unjust world systems and it choked the life out of them. It became perfectly clear to Caleb that he needed to stop waffling and say yes to the Shepherd's invitation.

∗∗∗

Once again, it was time for me to ask questions. As Caleb would often do, he wanted a woman's viewpoint before he gave his own. This time, he asked, "What do you see so far?"

"Stuck in my head are the Shulammite's words, 'I sought him, but did not find him; I called him, but he gave no answer.'[2] This feeling that God has gone missing, I feel it in my own life. Growing up in a fundamentalist church, that was focused on knowing and following the right rules, has left me feeling disconnected from God. Their rules—especially the ones that

---

2. Song 5:6.

banned women from full inclusion in the church—no longer made sense to me."

Caleb replied with, "God wasn't missing. You were just doing time in the harem."

"Can a church be an unjust system? Can the leaders be oppressors? Can the congregation be the harem?"

"Of course. You were resisting the unjust practices of that religious system. And it turned on you. Just like the girls in the harem turn on the Shulammite from time to time." Caleb went on to explain, "Those who resist unjust systems often have a sense of abandonment, but God has not left them. Doing time in the harem helps us see how bad the world is. It makes our choice clear: do we go along to get along or do we follow the Shepherd?"

It occurred to me that the Shulammite had gotten comfortable in the palace with her garments and fancy cosmetic lotions. She was falling in love with the fringe benefits. She was dreaming this time when the Shepherd shows up. She was in bed and could not be expected to get dressed again. When she decided to let him in, she no longer could, because the fancy lotions would not allow her to get a grip on the door handle. I asked Caleb if that is what he saw too.

He did and added, "It takes very little time to get comfortable in an unjust system—to get used to the golden handcuffs that the oppressor provides you. Soon, following the Shepherd becomes such an inconvenience that you can't even imagine that you're supposed to follow him. You'd have to give up too much. You even begin to reason that the Shepherd, who loves you, is the one who gave you these gifts and certainly wouldn't want you to give anything up!"

Reggie quoted Jesus, "'Whoever does not take up the cross and follow me is not worthy of me.'[3] Most of us aren't willing to take up the cross, because we've gotten cozy." Reggie's faith was authentic—nothing mushy about it. Despite the hiccup in our friendship, my admiration for him continued to grow.

Reggie went on. "There is something I think we're overlooking. It wasn't only the system at Grandville that was unjust. The system back home in Harrelson was unjust in its own ways too. There was corruption in Caleb's hometown among *his* people and even at Harrelson High. All world

3. Matt 10:38.

systems are corrupt. All human systems need to be restored to what God intended."

"It's hard to get my mind around," I admitted. "I want things to be cut and dry: Grandville bad and Harrelson good."

Reggie clarified, "When the Shepherd eventually leads her out of the harem back to their village, it isn't to a perfect place where all of her problems are solved. Do you remember her brothers? She told the harem early on that her brothers had overworked her because they were mad at her.[4] Getting to a perfect place isn't the point of the story."

"What is the point?"

"As the Shepherd leads her out of the harem, she leans on him. The villagers witness it and ask, 'Who is that coming up from the wilderness, leaning upon her beloved?'[5] I think that *leaning* on the Shepherd is the point," answered Reggie.

"Leaning?"

"Yes. She's no longer telling him what to do—to hide, to come back, to go away. She's leaning on him—putting her trust in him. That is the point. The Christian journey is not a search for the perfect village or the perfect church or the perfect theology. It is a journey into a deeper and deeper relationship with God where we lean on the Good Shepherd. It is then the Shepherd can use us to overcome the unjust systems in the world."

"And the unjust systems in the church?" I asked.

Reggie nodded.

"Enough. Reggie," Caleb laughed, "You are stealing the grand finale of my story! It must unfold for the woman."

Reggie laughed too and added, "Okay then. But let's get back to where we were. You weren't called to stay in Grandville and dismantle their unjust system. Yet, today you are called to dismantle unjust systems. You are helping the oppressed. You know, it always bothers me that you compare yourself to MLK Jr. unfavorably, because you are doing a lot of what MLK Jr. was all about."

"I don't know Reggie. MLK Jr. wasn't a politician—he was a minister. I am a politician. God focused MLK Jr. on African-American social issues. My call is to represent people in my district of all colors and faiths—and I take that very seriously. Therefore, I am not sure I accept that comparison. But I agree that God changed my calling over time."

4. Song 1:5–6.
5. Song 8:5.

14

Ridiculed

Song 5:9—6:9

SETTING: Halls of the country estate.

AT RISE: The SHULAMMITE has been summoned to KING
                SOLOMON's bedroom in the country estate. She does
                not want to go.

HAREM

(As the SHULAMMITE is walking to his bedroom, some of the women in the
HAREM follow her—taunting her.)

5:9 **What is your beloved more than another beloved, O fairest among
women? What is your beloved more than another beloved, that you thus
adjure us?**

SHULAMMITE

5:10 **My beloved is all radiant and ruddy, distinguished among ten
thousand.** 5:11 **His head is the finest gold; his locks are wavy, black as a raven.**[1] 5:12 **His eyes are like doves beside springs of water, bathed in milk,**

---

1. Smith, "Song of Solomon: Love Lost," disc 4. A head of gold represents great
noble character.

fitly set.[2] [5:13] His cheeks are like beds of spices, yielding fragrance. His lips are lilies, distilling liquid myrrh.[3] [5:14] His arms are rounded gold, set with jewels. His body is ivory work, encrusted with sapphires. [5:15] His legs are alabaster columns, set upon bases of gold. His appearance is like Lebanon, choice as the cedars. [5:16] His speech is most sweet, and he is altogether desirable. This is my beloved and this is my friend, O daughters of Jerusalem.

HAREM

(The HAREM continues to mock the SHULAMMITE.)

[6:1] Where has your beloved gone, O fairest among women? Which way has your beloved turned, that we may seek him with you?

SHULAMMITE

[6:2] My beloved has gone down to his garden, to the beds of spices, to pasture his flock in the gardens, and to gather lilies. [6:3] I am my beloved's and my beloved is mine; he pastures his flock among the lilies.[4,5]

(She reaches SOLOMON'S bedroom. He is waiting for her. The HAREM watches on from outside, curious what will happen when she rejects him. No one has ever rejected the King before.)

KING SOLOMON

(He wants to try and convince her one more time, but her constant rejection has started to frustrate him. He doesn't know how to deal with her any longer.)

---

2. Ibid., Disc 4. Doves represent innocence, tenderness, and simplicity.

3. Ibid., Disc 4. "Distilling liquid myrrh" means that his breath is sweet.

4. Tournay, *Word of God, Song of Love,* 86. This is the Abrahamic covenant formula. She has said it before in verse 2:16. Using this phrase here means that she desires to make the ultimate commitment to the Shepherd, entering into the marriage covenant with him.

5. Smith, "Song of Solomon: Love Lost," disc 4. The Shulammite is saying to the harem, "I haven't truly lost him—I know where he is." The garden represents one's innermost being in the Song. It is where we abide in him and he abides in us. Jesus said, "Abide in me as I abide in you" (John 15:4).

⁶:⁴ You are beautiful as Tirzah, my love, comely as Jerusalem, terrible as an army with banners.⁶,⁷ ⁶:⁵ Turn away your eyes from me, for they
overwhelm me!⁸ Your hair is like a flock of goats, moving down the slopes
of Gilead. ⁶:⁶ Your teeth are like a flock of ewes, that have come up from
the washing; all of them bear twins, and not one among them is bereaved.
⁶:⁷ Your cheeks are like halves of a pomegranate behind your veil. ⁶:⁸ There
are sixty queens and eighty concubines, and maidens without number.
⁶:⁹ My dove, my perfect one, is the only one, the darling of her mother,
flawless to her that bore her. The maidens saw her and called her happy;
the queens and concubines also, and they praised her.⁹

HAREM

(The HAREM sarcastically answers KING SOLOMON. They do not share his
admiration of the SHULAMMITE.)

⁶:¹⁰ "Who is this that looks forth like the dawn, fair as the moon,
bright as the sun, terrible as an army with banners?"¹⁰

***

When Caleb left the ICU to find a restroom, he found Rufus, Hallie,
and Jake sitting in the waiting room. It was impossible for him to look at
them. Rufus stood up and walked toward Caleb offering condolences, but

6. Tirzah was a beautiful city in Israel that meant "pleasant." Jerusalem was the city
around which everything in the Jewish world centered. By comparing her to Jerusalem,
he was saying to her that she is "regal" and "important."

7. "Terrible as an army with banners" described a threatening army advancing into
war. It was something to be respectfully afraid of—something not to be messed with.
Because she has gotten stronger and stronger at rejecting him, he was being pushed to
the point of giving up. This is what the Christian journey should be like—we should be
getting stronger and stronger in Christ.

8. Because Solomon can't seduce her, he realizes that he can't control her. He is
frustrated by the faithfulness exhibited toward her Shepherd. The covenant love she has
for the Shepherd has overcome him. He feels shabby in front of her.

9. Harper, "The Song of Solomon," 45. In this paragraph, Solomon is offering the
Shulammite first place in his harem. He is saying that she is worth more than all the other
women in the harem.

10. Smith, "Song of Solomon: Love Conquering," disc 5. The harem can see that the
King thinks of her as a force to be reckoned with. However, they don't share his admiration of her.

Caleb kept his head down and walked around Rufus without acknowledging him, stopping a few feet away at the reception desk to ask where the Negro restroom was located. It was in the basement.

He walked the stairs down to the basement. His heart pounding, his blood pressure soaring. Like most Negro restrooms, it was dark and needed major cosmetic attention. As he exited, in front of him stood Hallie.

"What are you doing here?" he asked coldly.

"Why are you so angry at us? We came to support you."

"I don't believe you, Hallie. I don't believe you at all." He wanted to hit something. Not her, but something. His anger was raging.

"So you're too good for our support? Well, let me tell you this. If you're so great and your God is so good, then where is your God now? Tell me that Caleb! Where was your God when your dad was getting beat up?"

Caleb turned away from her and faced the basement wall. There was a window well carved into the concrete block foundation. Through it he could see the sky. He could see bright clouds floating by. He watched them as he pondered what to say. As he did, his breathing changed. It slowed and calmed.

"I don't know why God let Doc get beat up. I don't know why God lets a lot of things happen. But I know that I am God's and God is mine. He's with Doc up in that hospital room and down here with me. And he wants to be with you."

Hallie's voice cracked as she spoke. "There was a church on the corner of the street I grew up on. My parents were too hung over from Saturday nights at the local bar to take me there. But on Sunday mornings, my friend and her family would stop by my house and walk with me to church. I followed all the church rules, but God didn't do anything for me. I was still the poorest kid in town with no one to take care of me. If there is a God, God doesn't care about me a bit. Not one bit. I had to make my own way."

"I'm sorry about your childhood, Hallie. It hurts me to think of you growing up alone or ever being mistreated. But it sounds like you followed some list of rules and thought that if you kept them, God would give you whatever you wanted. And when keeping the rules didn't buy you anything, then you hooked up with Jake so you could be important and have everything you wanted."

"I did. And it was a damn good choice. Look at me. I have nice clothes, a roof over my head, and a nice car to drive. What have you got?"

"I have the Creator of the universe—a God who loves me even when I screw up. I don't need anything else, Hallie." He turned around and looked at her, "You were right. I'm leaving Grandville."

He pushed by her in the stairwell and headed upstairs back to his father's room. Jake and Rufus were still waiting for him. Hallie joined them.

This time Caleb was ready for them. With a peace and calmness that is not humanly possible, he approached Rufus. As he did, Wade appeared from out of nowhere. He said nothing, but on cue, he appeared. He made sure Caleb saw him and then sat down in the corner of the waiting room slouched in a chair.

Before Caleb could open his mouth, Rufus said, "I don't want you to worry about the car. I had taken out insurance on it. You will have a new one and you can pick out any color you want."

"What? My dad is in there dying and you think I'm worried about a car?"

Despite the absurdity, Caleb remained calm and explained to Rufus that he could not accept the car. Rufus didn't argue. But he looked angry. His face turned red, his jaws were clenched.

Then Caleb really lowered the boom, "You also need to find a new coach."

"You don't know what you're doing son," expressed a beet red Rufus.

"No sir, I believe that I do."

This time Rufus turned his back on Caleb and walked out. Jake and Hallie didn't move. They stood there still staring at Caleb. Wade stayed seated in the corner. Caleb was not going to leave the room with Wade still in the hospital so he stood motionless staring at Wade in the corner of the room as he evaluated his options for removing him.

Then for the first time, Wade spoke. As clear as day with a deep raspy voice full of venom and hate, "How's your daddy?"

The look on the faces of Jake and Hallie took Caleb aback. Jake was embarrassed. Even though Jake never stood up to his family, he was ashamed of their behavior. Hallie was still reeling from their conversation in the basement. She was mad at Caleb. Caleb could see in her eyes that she was rooting for Doc to die. She wanted to see Caleb hurting worse than she wanted air in her lungs. Moreover, something about the way Rufus had just walked out told Caleb that Rufus was scared.

Scared.

Perhaps Rufus was scared because during the commotion over the car, the police had searched the locker room and found drugs in his grandson's bag. Maybe he was scared because he was afraid Caleb would testify against the boy. Maybe Rufus was afraid that Caleb's mom could ID Wade as the one who attacked Doc. But then again, Caleb doubted if Rufus cared what happened to Wade. Rufus might even welcome Wade's incarceration.

Caleb didn't have to think about what was going on for long. Rufus turned around and walked back in. He got right up in Caleb's face, "Son, I wasn't wild about bringing a Negro to Grandville. I'm not in favor of deseg-regation. But you were the best coach money could buy and I thought you could help me get my grandson into the big leagues. The problem with you is that you have no loyalty. No sense of your place."

Rufus took a long breath. Caleb thought Rufus was done, but he started up again, "To my surprise, people liked you—accepted you. The team liked you. Shoot, I even had to lean on my own grandson to get him to keep taking the damn amphetamines. He wanted to listen to your counsel, not mine. But without the drugs, the kid has no stamina. Without them he is just an average run of the mill player like," he pointed to Jake with his thumb as if he couldn't remember his name.

Jake closed his eyes and turned around with his back toward the group. Rufus went on, "I thought because—if nothing else—because you were a Negro, you'd be a little grateful that I would give you opportunities like no other black coach has ever had. But you have rejected my kindness."

"Kindness?" Caleb raised his voice as he leaned into Rufus. "My father is dying. And you have been kind to me?"

Hallie put her arm around Rufus's shoulder, "Rufus he isn't worth it. I don't know what you ever saw in him. Please. Let's get out of here."

***

Back in Caleb's DC office, Reggie had warned me that Caleb was go-ing to be interrupted by a visitor. Therefore, that was all the story I got that morning. The visitor waited while Caleb lingered for a couple of quick questions.

"Why was Rufus afraid?" I asked.

"Because he couldn't control me. He couldn't buy me with flattery, money, or fear."

"Does this mean he let you out of your contract?"

With one of his big smiles, Caleb answered, "Have patience, woman! Let me finish the story next week."

"Okay, but before you go, did you notice that the harem asks the Shulammite where her Shepherd is and she tells the women that he's in his garden?"

"Yes, she knows where he is now—he no longer feels missing to her. Throughout the song, the garden represents one's innermost place. But the harem—they don't get it. The harem, like most of us, wants a historically and geographically located Shepherd. But God is not historically and geographically located."

"Okay, but I expected her to tell them that he is in *her* garden—*her* innermost place—*her* heart. But she says he is in *his* garden not *her* garden."

"Oh, but his garden is her garden. Back in verse 4:16, she tells him that her garden is his garden. However, when she first said it, those were only words—an expression of her desire—but now she has truly let him in."

Caleb went to greet his visitor while Reggie and I finished up.

Reggie added, "Jesus said it this way, 'Abide in me, and I in you.'[11] The Shepherd's garden is within us—within our innermost parts. Yet, we are in his garden at the same time. It makes no sense in our physical world. But it is a theme that was important to Jesus. In fact, he says a similar thing about the Spirit."

> This is the Spirit of truth, whom the world cannot receive, because it neither sees him nor knows him. You know him, because he abides with you, and he will be in you. (John 14:17)

"This brings up something that I have wondered about on and off. Is the Shepherd a real physical presence in the story? Or is he a spirit? So far, no one has seen him but the Shulammite. Has he always been only in her heart?" I asked.

"I think you could argue either way. You could say that neither the harem nor the world can see him, because they are looking for a historically and geographically located Shepherd. However, in the end, the villagers do see him. They see her leaning on him. Still you could argue that they see him because they, like the Shulammite, know him. Not because he's physically present."

Clarifying, I asked, "Either way, would you agree that the important point is that when we say yes to letting Christ into our garden—this place

11. John 15:4.

deep within us—it is then that we can have our most intimate fellowship with him?"

"Absolutely," concluded Reggie.

Another well spent Sunday morning. I gathered my things and said good-bye to Reggie. Caleb had gone somewhere with his visitor and was nowhere to be seen. I only got a few steps into the hall when Reggie caught up to me.

"I owe you an explanation," he said gently.

"No you don't. I would like to go back to being friends though." My words came out less breezy than I had hoped and more like begging.

"Deal. I want you to know that I like you and not just as a friend. But it can't go any further."

The look on my face immediately went from upbeat to frustrated. "Why did you have to tell me that? Why did you want me to know that you liked me? Couldn't you have let well enough alone and just let us be friends? Now you do owe me an explanation!" I had long passed acting breezy and nonchalant.

"I can't get involved with a white girl."

"Why not?"

"It would kill my parents." The pain on his face was evident. This was something that he had put considerable thought into and was resolved about. "You don't know what it is like being black—what we go through every day in this country. My family would see it as a rejection of them and of our culture—of all that we have struggled for. They are expecting me to marry a black girl. They are expecting black grandchildren. It would be a betrayal."

My hackles were up now. "First of all, I didn't ask you to *marry* me. I just wanted to go for a walk. Second, what kind of unjust system insists you marry someone because of the color of their skin and not because you love them?"

Reggie had expected me to understand, not get angrier. Why I was getting angrier wasn't immediately clear to me either, but I was too angry to continue a civil conversation.

Caleb rounded the hall and saw us standing there. "Is everything okay?" he asked.

"Yes!" we said in unison.

"I see," said Caleb unconvinced. As he narrowed in on us, he repeated, "Oh . . . I see." He was too wise not to realize that there was more to our relationship than he had previously been aware. Not intending to minimize the pain evident on both of our faces, a knowing smile slipped onto his lips.

I used the interruption to make it to the stairwell and out the door. As I hit the streets to walk home, I hoped beyond hope that Reggie would pull up next to me in his car once again, but he didn't. I made it all the way home, collapsed on my couch, and cried until I fell asleep—napping restlessly on and off until dinner. I understood that dating a white woman might look like a betrayal to other African-Americans. I truly did. I wasn't uncompassionate about his feelings at all. But at the same time, why did I have to like him so much? It was an injustice that I had never anticipated.

God in our Dreams

The Shulammite's deepest thoughts came to her while she was on the verge of sleep. There are many occasions in Scripture where God speaks to people through their dreams. God used the imagery of stars and sheaves to tell Joseph he would rule over his brothers.[1] Jacob saw a ladder that reached into heaven.[2] God used the imagery of a statue to tell Nebuchadnezzar that he and his kingdom were in trouble.[3] In the Old Testament and again in the New Testament, it was written that when the Holy Spirit is given, "old men will dream dreams."[4] Dreaming was once an expected way of God speaking, but not something we talk about very much today.

In this section of verses, the Shulammite has had a nightmare.[5] This dream serves to inform her about the dangers of sending the Shepherd away. The dream will propel her toward accepting his invitation to follow him.

How to Look for God in our Dreams

Dreaming is something that happens every night to every human. Sometimes we remember our dreams and sometimes we don't. Sometimes God speaks in them. When God chooses to speak through a dream is up

1. Gen 37.
2. Gen 28:12.
3. Dan 2.
4. Joel 2:28 and Acts 2:17.
5. Song 5:2–8.

to God, but we can be ready and open to it. In our sleep, there are no distractions so it makes sense that God would take advantage of this time to engage us. Some people believe that God even speaks into the dreams that we don't remember. These people often report that they simply have a sense of comfort that God was watching over them during the night. To practice this discipline:

- Take your journal (or possibly a tape recorder) to bed with you and be prepared to record your dreams as soon as you wake up even if it is in the middle of the night. Most people do not remember their dreams if they do not record them right away.

- Just before you fall asleep, tell God that you are open to being spoken to in your dreams.

Day 1–3 Dreaming with Scripture

- Pick a verse or story from the Bible to meditate on as you fall asleep. You can do different meditations each night or the same one every night.

- In the morning, immediately upon waking, read the verse or story you were meditating on the night before.

- Was anything new revealed to you as you slept? Journal.

Day 4–5 Freestyle Dreaming

- On these days, you do not meditate before sleeping. However, don't forget to pray before you go to sleep asking God to be present in your dreams. Dream, journal, and go right back to sleep.

- In the morning, read your journal. Meditate on your dream and any feelings that come to you when you wake. Did God speak through the dream? Did the dream tell you something about what is going on in your subconscious? Did it tell you something about your journey with God? Journal.

- If you can't remember any dreams, journal about how you felt upon wakening.

ACT 6

Love Wins

For to this you have been called, because Christ also suffered for you, leaving you an example, so that you should follow in his steps. "He committed no sin, and no deceit was found in his mouth." When he was abused, he did not return abuse; when he suffered, he did not threaten; but he entrusted himself to the one who judges justly. He himself bore our sins in his body on the cross, so that, free from sins, we might live for righteousness; by his wounds you have been healed. For you were going astray like sheep, but now you have returned to the shepherd and guardian of your souls.

—1 Peter 2:21–25

15

Rejecting the Oppressor
Song 6:13—7:10

SETTING: The entrance to KING SOLOMON's country estate.

AT RISE: The VILLAGERS from the SHULAMMITE's hometown of Shulem have heard that the SHULAMMITE is at KING SOLOMON's estate. They have gathered at the entrance to see her.

VILLAGERS

(The VILLAGERS form a chorus calling her to come to where they can see her.)

6:13 **Return, return, O Shulammite! Return, return, that we may look upon you.**

SHULAMMITE

(She hears the VILLAGERS from a balcony of the palace and cries to them.)

Why should you look upon the Shulammite?

VILLAGERS

As upon a dance before two armies.[1] [7:1] How graceful are your feet in sandals, O queenly maiden! Your rounded thighs are like jewels, the work of a master hand.[2] [7:2] Your navel is a rounded bowl that never lacks mixed wine. Your belly is a heap of wheat, encircled with lilies.[3] [7:3] Your two breasts are like two fawns, twins of a gazelle. [7:4] Your neck is like an ivory tower. Your eyes are pools in Heshbon, by the gate of Bath-rabbim. Your nose is like a tower of Lebanon, overlooking Damascus. [7:5] Your head crowns you like Carmel, and your flowing locks are like purple; a king is held captive in the tresses.

KING SOLOMON

(KING SOLOMON appears and makes one last appeal to the SHULAMMITE.)

[7:6] How fair and pleasant you are, O loved one, delectable maiden! [7:7] You are stately as a palm tree, and your breasts are like its clusters. [7:8] I say I will climb the palm tree and lay hold of its branches. Oh, may your breasts be like clusters of the vine, and the scent of your breath like apples, [7:9] and your kisses like the best wine that goes down smoothly, gliding over lips and teeth.

SHULAMMITE

(Rejects KING SOLOMON.)

[7:10] I am my beloved's, and his desire is for me.

---

1. The villagers say that looking upon the Shulammite is like looking "upon a dance before two armies." She is in a struggle between the King and the Shepherd—a struggle between her oppressor and her Creator—a struggle between unjust systems and the Kingdom of God.

2. It is interesting to note how many interpretations of this verse could be considered sexist. Instead of joining with the villagers to celebrate the Shulammite's ample thighs, many interpreters have rewritten their praises to say "curves of the hips" or "graceful legs." The Hebrew word means "the fleshy portion of the upper thigh." Let's take a moment to celebrate the beauty of women who have ample thighs!

3. Let's take another moment to celebrate the beauty of women whose bellies are like a "heap of wheat!" The beautiful Shulammite had ample thighs and a big rounded tummy! May all women with ample thighs and curvy tummies know they too are beautiful!

***

To my surprise, Reggie called and asked me to grab breakfast with him before meeting with Caleb that Sunday morning. Upon arrival at the Capitol Hill restaurant, I blurted out immediately that I no longer needed an explanation about what couldn't be changed, but I did want to find a way to be friends.

He responded, "I'm fine with that for now."

His words, "for now," hung in the air, but I pretended not to notice. I had decided after much internal commotion of my own that his friendship was all there would ever be and that I would make myself okay with that.

Breakfast was fine. The restaurant was the haunt of many famous politicians. Usually, whenever I ate there, it was hard for me to stop staring at the door hoping to spot some important person's arrival, but because I was worried about the dynamics between Reggie and me, the President could have walked in and I wouldn't have noticed. I was also tired. I had laid awake until the early morning hours planning what I would say to Reggie. In the end, I thought it best just to talk about Caleb's story and let things get back to normal.

I started the conversation with something we had touched on before, "We've talked about how the Shulammite turned King Solomon away by remembering her Shepherd. We've talked about how she uses the Abrahamic covenant formula, 'I am his and he is mine,' to declare her commitment to the Shepherd. But I don't think we've ever mentioned that she is also always offering praises to her Shepherd. What do you make of that?"

He laughed and with a tone of disappointment said, "Okay, we'll talk about the Shulammite." Reggie was partly amused and partly frustrated that I didn't want to talk about "our" situation. Fortunately, my prompt reminded him of a story from the early days of the church.

> After the authorities had given Paul and Silas a severe flogging, they threw them into prison and ordered the jailer to keep them securely. Following these instructions, he put them in the innermost cell and fastened their feet in the stocks. About midnight Paul and Silas were praying and singing hymns to God, and the prisoners were listening to them. Suddenly there was an earthquake, so violent that the foundations of the prison were shaken; and immediately all the doors were opened and everyone's chains were unfastened. (Acts 16:23–26)

Reggie reasoned that the normal thing for Paul and Silas to have done would have been to devise some sort of plan to get out of prison by either hiring a lawyer, bribing the jailer, or just plain figuring out how to escape. Instead, Paul and Silas praised God. The result was that God fought their battle for them with an earthquake.

"Now how do you know the earthquake was sent by God and not just a happy coincidence?" I challenged.

"Well, I imagine an earthquake might shake the doors off their hinges. But this one unfastened their chains. That has got to be God," answered Reggie. He folded his arms in pretend smugness at coming up with a quick answer to my challenge. "By the way, that isn't the only Scripture where our praises connect us in some supernatural way to God."

He told me of another verse, this one in Psalm 22:3. It describes the same sort of mystical relationship between God and our praises. It says that God inhabits (or is enthroned upon) the praises of God's people.

This stirred in me another long forgotten story from my Sunday school days as a child. In the Old Testament, there was a battle to be waged, but God tells the ancient Jews not to fight:

> This battle is not for you to fight; take your position, stand still, and see the victory of the LORD on your behalf. (2 Chr 20:17)

The next day, God gives them specific instructions to send the choir onto the battlefield where they will sing God's praises. They never lift a hand against the enemy and the enemy ends up destroying itself. Scripture points to something—something mystical—about praising God that helps us resist. Even in the wilderness when Jesus was being tempted by the devil Jesus finally says, "Worship the Lord your God, and serve only him."[4] It is then the devil finally leaves him and angels come to wait upon Jesus.

I wondered out loud, "Could it be that when we praise God unjust systems lose their grip on us?"

"Yes! I think that is a key point in the Song," said Reggie.

By the time we got the check, breakfast felt like a success. Reggie was acting like his old self and I was successfully managing my disappointment. However, our meeting with Caleb afterwards was unexpectedly emotional.

4. Matt 4:10–11.

***

Back at the hospital in Harrelson, Doc shocked everyone the next morning by coming out of his coma. Caleb and his mom were sitting by Doc's bed looking out the window at a Georgia thrasher that had perched nearby. The brown bird was large even for a thrasher—maybe a foot long. It was singing to another thrasher, unseen somewhere nearby. The two birds were making a beautiful song together.

Caleb and his mom were both lost in thought, when without warning Doc quoted, from all things, the Song of Solomon. Well, it was sort of the Song of Solomon: "The time of singing has come and the voice of the Georgia thrasher is heard in the land."

Caleb's mom ran for the nurse while Caleb stayed at his dad's side and held his hand. His dad's eyes had not opened. Caleb didn't know if Doc was dying and these were to be his last words or if he was coming back to life. It was a tense few minutes while he waited for his mother to find the nurse. It seemed to take forever. It must have seemed like forever to Doc too, because Doc—still without opening his eyes—spoke again, "Now where did that woman go?" Caleb knew then that Doc was going to be okay.

The doctors called it nothing short of miraculous. Nevertheless, Caleb was riddled with guilt. In the days that followed, Caleb retraced his steps trying to figure out where he had gone wrong. Not only had he taken a job for pure greed, but he had put the people he loved in harm's way. He revisited the events of the entire misadventure over and over starting with the job interview. He realized that Hallie and her team had presented him with a trumped-up picture of what coaching at Grandville would be like. Yet, they hadn't really fooled him. In his heart, he had known something was wrong all along. He had been so tired of everything. He was tired of being a widower. He was tired of babysitting poverty-stricken teenagers. The Grandville job interview had presented him with a way out—a way that he could have all the stuff that he had never been able to have. So he jumped at the chance to have fancy things.

He was so ashamed. He had made that decision with no regard for the call God had placed on his life to minister to those Harrelson kids. He had had no regard for the love his parents had shown him and all that they had taught him. It had been a despicable decision. There was a giant rip in his heart. And worst of all, he didn't know what to do next.

Caleb's mom knew what was going on in Caleb's heart. She knew he was beating himself up and she couldn't watch him suffer. She got in his face just like she had that day in the school hallway and put one hand on each shoulder, "Now son, I want you to listen to me. You are not responsible for what happened to your father. A bad man hurt your father—not you. But son, you need to let God speak to you and find out what your next steps are. You can't keep traveling around in the dark."

"But I willingly took this job! Mom, I don't understand how I could be so foolish."

"So ask God to forgive you. But more importantly, you have to accept God's forgiveness. It's a sin to hold onto guilt. It will hold you back from being all God wants you to be."

His mom went on to name all the Bible characters she could think of who had pulled themselves together and made something out of themselves after accepting God's forgiveness. There was King David, rapist and murderer. He accepted God's forgiveness and went back to serving God as King.[5] The Apostle Paul, murderer and persecutor of Christians, went on to write most of the New Testament.[6] The Apostle Peter, who denied even knowing Christ at Christ's trial, went on to be the head of the church.[7]

"Son, if you keep this guilt up, it means you aren't leaning on the power and the grace of God to carry you forward. If you are truly sorry, then you must give up the guilt so you can follow Jesus."

That day, Caleb made his way to the little white wooden church Doc had preached in every Sunday for decades. The bright red doors were always open so Caleb made his way inside. The wooden floors creaked as he knelt in the back and asked for forgiveness.

***

Caleb could not tell this part of his story without tears washing down his black face. How beautiful his wrinkled old face really was. It almost glowed. I could not watch Caleb be so moved without feeling both his pain and his joy so I cried along with him.

"In that little church, I asked God to take away the guilt I felt and to make me strong enough to do whatever God had planned for me—no matter how hard," Caleb remembered. "In the light of the simple stained glass window, I went from saying yes to the Good Shepherd with my words to

5. 2 Sam 12—11.

6. Acts 26.

7. Matt 26:69–75.

truly giving myself up so that the Good Shepherd could use me." He paused to wipe away tears. Then when he could speak again, he said, "It was there that the garden of the Good Shepherd and my garden became one and the same."

Caleb stopped talking and looked at me. He breathed a sigh of relief. After a few moments of complete silence, I realized that he seemed to think he was finished with his story.

"And?" I asked.

"That's it."

"What do you mean? The end of the story?" I was confused. This was not the end of his story!

"Yes. Think about it. It doesn't matter what happened after that. I had finally said yes to the Shepherd with my whole heart. In doing so, Rufus and the harem had no further hold on me. I was ready to go—or stay—wherever the Good Shepherd would lead me. This is what the Song is about."

"But Caleb, you have to explain what you've been doing since that day."

"Dismantling injustices of every kind."

"Keep explaining." I ordered.

"Every time we say yes to the Good Shepherd instead of the oppressor, the oppressor's unjust systems lose their destructive hold on us and we are free to experience the Good Shepherd's perfect and nurturing love. It's then we have the power to do whatever God calls us to do—to face whatever unjust system is before us, call it out, and let God use us to dismantle it."

"But how? Explain what you do next to dismantle it."

"It's different every time. I don't know until the Good Shepherd leads me. I tell God all about it, I wait for God to speak, and then I move forward. Sometimes I confront the oppressor with logic and education. Sometimes I form a march or a sit-in. Sometimes I introduce a bill. I never know what God will tell me to do until God speaks. The Song of Solomon teaches us how to dismantle our internal holdups keeping us from intimacy with God. Once those are dismantled, we are free to hear the instructions from God. Because I said yes to the Shepherd, I abide in Christ and Christ in me. Therefore, I have access to wisdom and power that I wouldn't have had otherwise."

"Do you ever get it wrong?"

"Are you asking if I'm human? Of course," laughed Caleb. "However, I now know how to get to the garden where the Good Shepherd lives," as he spoke, he pointed to his heart. "I didn't know how to do that before I went to Grandville and lived in the harem for a while."

"Ok, Caleb." I said, determined to get more. "I understand how this is the end of your story as it relates to the Shulammite. But you must tell me what happened the days and weeks following your prayer in Doc's church—how it led you to be one of the most powerful leaders in this great country of ours."

Caleb smiled, looked at Reggie, and continued his story.

✳✳✳

After Doc's recovery in the hospital, Caleb didn't return to Grandville for two weeks while he helped his mom get his dad situated. They took Doc to the converted home of a sympathetic white nurse who offered physical therapy to recovering patients. As an admirer of Doc's ministry, she accepted not a penny of payment. Her place was a huge, pleasant old house full of joy and hope. Doc was to stay there until he could get around on his own.

By now, everyone in Harrelson had come to see Doc. Everyone in town had also begged Caleb to come home for good. Caleb longed for his old job, but they had hired a replacement. The job was no longer open and jobs were very scarce in Harrelson.

Caleb kept asking himself what God was doing. Was God going to make him stay in Grandville after all—this time being the true example God wanted him to be? If so, then why could Caleb no longer stand the thought of going back? Caleb spent many early mornings sitting in the church waiting for God to speak.

Then one afternoon, Caleb pushed Doc's wheelchair into the court-yard of the house and sat with him. Together, they breathed in the warm fresh air. Both of them were exhausted. They fell in and out of sleep as they sat there together. It wasn't long until Caleb was startled by a shadow falling over him. Someone was standing behind him. It frightened Caleb. Caleb immediately rose from his chair and swung around to confront the owner of the shadow. But it was only the principal of Harrelson High. He was a short wiry man with boundless energy. He greeted both of them with hardy handshakes.

Doc thanked the principal for coming to see him.

"I didn't come to see you Doc!" teased the principal.

178

"You didn't? Well, I'm hurt then," laughed Doc.

"Shoot. I know you're gonna be fine. You don't need any visitors. But Caleb does. I came to see him."

"You did?" both Caleb and his dad answered in unison as Caleb sat back down.

"Yes. I came to see Caleb. As you know, we've filled your old position. So I came to tell you that you've been replaced." Caleb's heart sank. He knew it already, but hearing it hurt.

While Caleb began to sulk, Doc snorted. "I know you didn't come here to tell him that."

"True. But I wanted to make Caleb suffer a bit!" The clothing on the short, skinny principal shook as he laughed again.

"Why did you come?" asked Caleb too emotionally torn by the events of the last few weeks to see that he was being teased.

"We have an opening for a political science teacher. If you took it, I might—and *might* is the operative word here—ask the new guy to let you coach a little in your free time."

"Noooo kidding!" said Doc as if he had been expecting it all along. Miracles for Doc were just a way of life.

"No kidding?" probed Caleb.

"We need you here Caleb. You helped these boys see beyond their circumstances. You built character in them. You were an example to them of what a man should be."

"Well, I haven't been much of an example lately. I ran off to take this job based on nothing but greed. I told everyone I was taking it to make strides in desegregation. But it was greed."

"You don't owe me an explanation, Caleb. But I want to make you this offer. As your potential employer, I ask you to consider it thoughtfully. As an elder at Doc's church, I ask you to pray about it."

"Thank you. I will ask God to make the decision clear to me. You pray for me too." Unexpectedly, the short little principal got on one knee to the side of Caleb's chair and with his arm on Caleb's back, he prayed out loud with a booming voice that shook the trees in the courtyard. The man was little, but everything he did was big.

The following Monday, Caleb returned to Grandville. He had no sooner walked into his old office than the school secretary came to get him. She said there was a visitor for him. He didn't ask who and she didn't offer.

He took time to look over his schedule for the day and walked down to the office.

It was no surprise that it was Rufus. Rufus was standing in the athletic director's office with his hat in hand—literally. Rufus apologized to Caleb for everything—what had happened to Doc, for offering him the car, for the angry words he had said at the hospital. Then he got real honest with Caleb, "I paid the school to bring you here in hopes that you would coach my grandson and give him every chance possible to get into the big leagues. He is a junior this year and will be a senior next. I want to ask you—for his sake, not mine—that you stay until he graduates and teach him everything you can. You're the man to give him the best shot conceivable."

"Rufus, I think we both know that isn't possible." Caleb spoke unflinchingly.

Rufus began with the flattery again. But Caleb had heard enough. "Rufus, my life belongs to God. God wants me with the kids at Harrelson."

***

"Did they ever make an arrest in the attack on your father?" I inquired.

"Of course not," said Caleb with a hint of sarcasm. "The sheriff tried his best to find witnesses and no one would come forward."

"But I thought your mom saw Wade in the act."

"No one would take the word of a black woman over Rufus. Rufus had most certainly paid people off to say Wade was with them at the time. To add insult to injury the sheriff lost in the next election."

"Rufus's arms actually did reach that far?" I was floored.

"Well, the sheriff ran again the following election and won. That meant Rufus eventually lost his reach."

"How did Rufus's grandson turn out? Did he make the big leagues?"

"Nope. He died in a car crash his senior year. He was driving a nice new shiny blue car."

"No!" I couldn't believe it.

"Yes. I never saw Rufus again," said Caleb shaking his head.

"So there was no fixing that unjust system?"

"The Good Shepherd can fix all unjust systems. But I wasn't the one he was going to work through to fix that one."

"What happened to Jake and Hallie?"

180

"Jake left Hallie for the redhead after their son's death. Rufus took the death so hard that I heard he sold the lodge near Harrelson and disappeared once and for all into his house in Grandville. He closed his office and gave away those Scottish standing stones to be placed in a local park."

It was funny to be reminded of Rufus's odd obsession with Scotland. Yet, the story was too sad to laugh.

"Did you ever think Rufus might change?"

"No. But I do believe that King Solomon changed."

"Really?" I couldn't imagine that the Don Juan of Jerusalem would ever have had a reason to change his ways. I pointed out that even King Solomon's last words to the Shulammite showed he was still up to his same old tricks.

"True. However, the Song of Solomon wasn't the end of Solomon's story. The book of Ecclesiastes was attributed to him too.[8] Ecclesiastes was written about the end of Solomon's life. The Solomon in Ecclesiastes was a man who had turned from seeking self-fulfillment all his life to finally realizing the key to a purposeful life was seeking God. He wrote that his life had been pointless: 'All is vanity' or 'Wind, wind, empty wind.'[9] Life for Solomon had been like chasing the wind until, at the very end of his life, he decided to seek God instead."

Later I found the Scripture that Caleb referred to. It was very similar to the lyrical style of Song of Solomon.

> Remember your Creator in the days of your youth, before the days of trouble come, and the years draw near when you will say, "I have no pleasure in them"; before the sun and the light and the moon and the stars are darkened and the clouds return with the rain; in the day when the guards of the house tremble, and the strong men are bent, and the women who grind cease working because they are few, and those who look through the windows see dimly; when the doors on the street are shut, and the sound of the grinding is low, and one rises up at the sound of a bird, and all the daughters of song are brought low; when one is afraid of heights, and terrors are in the road; the almond tree blossoms, the grasshopper drags itself along and desire fails; because all must go to their eternal home, and the mourners will go about the streets; before the silver

8. According to rabbinic tradition, the Song of Solomon, Proverbs, and Ecclesiastes were written either by King Solomon or about him, where the Song was written early in his life, Proverbs in his middle years, and Ecclesiastes in his old age.

9. Eccl 1:2, 17.

cord is snapped, and the golden bowl is broken, and the pitcher is broken at the fountain, and the wheel broken at the cistern, and the dust returns to the earth as it was, and the breath returns to God who gave it . . . Fear God, and keep his commandments; for that is the whole duty of everyone. For God will bring every deed into judgment, including every secret thing, whether good or evil. (Eccl 12:1–14)

Caleb believed that Ecclesiastes explained what Solomon had learned in his old age—that his life had no meaning unless God was the center of it. Solomon had tried everything to make himself happy—he had even tried to enslave the Shulammite. For Caleb, Ecclesiastes was a work that flowed from Solomon's repentance and confession. Caleb found great hope in this—a hope that he extended to every oppressor.

Caleb explained, "Back then, I was grieving so much over the part I had played in my father's injuries that I saw Rufus as Satan himself. However, later, when I read Ecclesiastes, I realized that even King Solomon was human and capable of having a change of heart. Ecclesiastes has been a lesson to me not to give up on the Rufus's of the world. They may be responsible for unjust systems that hurt many people, but God loves them. There is still hope for them. God is that big."

"I can see that attitude of not giving up on others has served you well in politics."

"Indeed. I never approach the oppressor as if he or she is hopeless. I approach them with hope and the knowledge that the Good Shepherd loves them too. I assume that they can be educated. I always hope that someday they will come around. In fact, I try to make it easy for them to change."

"The truth, Caleb, is that they rarely do," interjected Reggie. Then to me, he added, "Caleb has a far higher view of the ability of people to change than I do."

"Three things, Reggie," started Caleb, "First, the oppressor's story isn't over until it's over. Sometimes it takes years for a transformation to occur. Second, while oppressors can't change themselves, God can. Third, just because I have hope for the oppressor, doesn't mean I don't still speak truth about their unjust systems. It is very much a tough love situation."

Caleb smiled at Reggie. Reggie lifted one eyebrow as if to say, "Maybe." Caleb was a wise and patient old teacher!

16

Commitment to the Shepherd

Song 7:11—8:14

SETTING: The road into the SHULAMMITE's hometown.

AT RISE: The SHULAMMITE has been set free. She is leaving KING SOLOMON's country estate and walking to her village. She calls to her SHEPHERD who she can see coming for her. The HAREM is standing with her.

SHULAMMITE

(SHULAMMITE calls to the SHEPHERD.)

^{7:11} **Come, my beloved, let us go forth into the fields, and lodge in the villages;** ^{7:12} **let us go out early to the vineyards, and see whether the vines have budded, whether the grape blossoms have opened and the pomegranates are in bloom. There I will give you my love.** ^{7:13} **The mandrakes give forth fragrance, and over our doors are all choice fruits, new as well as old, which I have laid up for you, O my beloved.** ^{8:1} **O that you were like a brother to me, who nursed at my mother's breast! If I met you outside, I would kiss you, and no one would despise me.**[1] ^{8:2} **I would lead you and bring you into the house of my mother, and into the chamber of the one**

---

1. Soughers, *Falling in Love with God*, 131–32. It was against Jewish law for a woman to kiss a man that was not her husband, father, son, or brother. She is saying, "I wish you were my brother so that I could kiss you right now!"

who bore me.[2] I would give you spiced wine to drink, the juice of my pomegranates. [8:3] O that his left hand were under my head, and that his right hand embraced me!

(The SHULAMMITE warns the HAREM once last time.)

[8:4] I adjure you, O daughters of Jerusalem, do not stir up or awaken love until it is ready!

(The SHULAMMITE leans on her SHEPHERD as they walk to their village.)

VILLAGERS

[8:5] Who is that coming up from the wilderness, leaning upon her beloved?[3]

SHULAMMITE

(Speaking to her SHEPHERD.)

Under the apple tree, I awakened you.[4] There your mother was in labor with you; there she who bore you was in labor. [8:6] Set me as a seal upon your heart, as a seal upon your arm; for love is strong as death, passion

---

2. Bringing him into her mother's house represents the ultimate commitment to the Shepherd.

3. Smith, "Song of Solomon: Love Triumphant," disc 6. "Leaning upon her beloved" can also be translated "leaning *completely* upon her beloved." *Leaning on* her beloved is the point—not *leaving with* her beloved. Leaning completely on him shows that she is no longer resisting Solomon's unjust system on her own, but trusting in her Shepherd. While it is possible that God calls us at times to resist and work for change from within the harem without leaving it, that too is only possible if we lean completely on God.

4. Theodoret of Cyrus, *Interpretatio*, is referenced in Norris, *Song of Songs*, 281. Though the tree in the Garden of Eden was not a specific type of tree, it is not hard to see the similarities and differences between the tree in the Garden of Eden and this apple tree. In the garden, humanity died from eating fruit of the forbidden tree. Here, under the apple tree, there is a birth, an awakening, or even a resurrection.

fierce as the grave.[5,6] Its flashes are flashes of fire, a raging flame.[7] [8:7] Many waters cannot quench love, neither can floods drown it. If one offered for love all the wealth of his house, it would be utterly scorned.

VILLAGERS

(The VILLLAGERS meet the SHULAMMITE bringing with them a young GIRL, who may someday face a similar ordeal. They ask the SHULAMMITE for wisdom.)

[8:8] We have a little sister, and she has no breasts.[8] What shall we do for our sister, on the day when she is spoken for?[9] [8:9] If she is a wall, we will build upon her a battlement of silver; but if she is a door, we will enclose her with boards of cedar.[10]

SHULAMMITE

(Speaking to the GIRL.)

---

5. A seal upon the heart represents a private knowledge and commitment to one another. A seal upon the arm represent a public commitment to each other.

6. "Love as strong as death" could also be interpreted "Love as inevitable as death." She is saying that she can't escape his love. In John Calvin's *Commentary on John* (John 6:41–45), he says, "The Holy Spirit is irresistible." In the same way, the Shulammite is saying the Shepherd is irresistible.

7. "A raging fire" can also be translated as "a fire that is never consumed." God's love is an eternal flame. In Exod 3:2, the voice of God is described as coming from a "flame of fire out of a bush . . . the bush was blazing, yet it was not consumed." God is love, which means God's love is eternal and never burns out. Ginsburg, *Song of Songs*, 188, writes that these flames emanate from the eternal source of all love.

8. Ginsburg, *Song of Songs*, 189. "Having no breasts," meant that she was too young for marriage.

9. Exum, *Song of Songs*, 257–58. "What shall we do for our sister, on the day when she is spoken for?" can also be translated "What do we do for our sister on the day that it is told of her?" The implication is that they are asking how they can make sure that she will remain chaste when she is tempted.

10. Pope, *Song of Songs*, 679–82. If she is a wall, it means she will resist the oppressor and they can even use her as a foundation for their protection. If she is a door, she will give in to the oppressor and they will protect her with cedar boards. Cedar is a strong wood.

8:10 I was a wall, and my breasts were like towers; then I was in his eyes as one who brings peace.[11] 8:11 Solomon had a vineyard at Baal-hamon; he entrusted the vineyard to keepers; each one was to bring for its fruit a thousand pieces of silver. 8:12 My vineyard, my very own, is for myself; you, O Solomon, may have the thousand, and the keepers of the fruit two hundred!

SHEPHERD

8:13 O you who dwell in the gardens, my companions are listening for your voice; let me hear it.[12]

SHULAMMITE

8:14 Make haste, my beloved, and be like a gazelle or a young stag upon the mountains of spices!

＊

Caleb's job at Harrelson didn't start until the fall so he spent his summer taking his father to physical therapy, relearning political science, and getting his classes ready for the fall. It would be nice if Caleb's story had an immediate happy ending. I would like to write that Caleb's salary was increased tenfold, he found a new love back at Harrelson, segregation truly ended once and for all, and he lived a fairytale life. Well, it didn't happen like that—except, he continued through good and bad to experience God's great love. As the Shulammite knew, the love of God for Caleb (for all of us) was as:

> Strong as death, passion fierce as the grave. Its flashes are flashes of fire, a raging flame. Many waters cannot quench love, neither can floods drown it. (Song 8:6–7)

---

11. Smith, "Song of Solomon: Love Triumphant," disc 6. "Peace" is the Hebrew word *shalom* that means wholeness or completeness. When she resisted the oppressor, he then saw her as one who was whole and complete—one whom he could not compromise.

12. This may be the most beautiful and poetical statement of the mission of the followers of the Shepherd. On behalf of the Good Shepherd, we listen for those who are calling to him and intercede for them.

The eternal love that God has for us is everything that we will ever need. Caleb found it was all he needed. Having wealth or "fancy things," as Caleb had always put it, did not compare to letting oneself experience the love of the Creator. The Shulammite agreed with him on this:

> If one offered for love all the wealth of his house, it would be utterly scorned. (Song 8:7)

In truth, Caleb went back to living near the poverty line, coaching teens who desperately needed him to be there for them, and winning baseball championships. Not every teen whom he worked with turned out okay. There were many problems—not a few caused by horrific injustices against African-Americans. Hours were long and money was short. To the outsider, nothing much had changed. Caleb was still underpaid and underappreciated. But he had not gone back to Harrelson High because he thought that all of the problems had been worked out. He had gone back because it was where the Good Shepherd had led him. It was where he would find *his* purpose and fulfilment. It was where he could live out the Kingdom of God on earth. It was there that, as commanded by the last words of the Good Shepherd to the Shulammite, he listened for the voice of those in need and interceded for them:

> O you who dwell in the gardens, my companions are listening for your voice; let me hear it. (Song 8:13)

What he went back to Harrelson with was far more important than what he had left with. He now knew how to be in relationship with God—how to pray, how to make space to listen, how to follow, and how to give himself up to God and others in holy service. Most importantly, he stopped kidding himself that he could align himself with an unjust system and still have an authentic relationship with God. These skills and lessons would later follow him into public office.

The Shulammite had said that Solomon grew to see her as "one who brings *shalom*." I understood this to mean that she had successfully resisted the temptations that Solomon had placed before her. Therefore, he saw her as possessing a wholeness (the full meaning of *shalom*) that he could never break down. But I wanted to get Caleb's take on this.[13]

---

13. Harper, *The Song of Solomon*, 60 and Godet, "The Interpretation of the Song of Songs," in Kaiser, *Classical Evangelical Essays in Old Testament Interpretation*,163. Harper and Godet have yet another interpretation. Solomon was forced to deal with the Shulammite like a city he could not capture. Left with no alternative, he made peace with her by

Although he didn't disagree with my theory, he remembered how his father had taught these verses. His father contrasted the way that the Shulammite made peace—a combination of peaceful resistance, praise to God, and truth telling—with something that Doc had called "The Trickster."

It turns out that "The Trickster" was a common archetype in stories coming from the slave plantations of the South. Br'er Rabbit, a story my own Southern grandmother had told me as a child, was a famous example.[14] But there were many trickster stories. The Br'er Rabbit story goes like this: Briar Rabbit, caught in a trap pleads with the Fox, who has trapped him, to set him free.

Caleb put on a heavy southern accent as he recalled what the rabbit said to the fox, "Please, Br'er Fox, don't fling me in dat brier-patch." Of course, the mean despicable Fox wanted nothing more than to do exactly what the Rabbit feared most. So he freed the Rabbit and flung him into the brier-patch. Since rabbits are at home in brier-patches, the resourceful Br'er Rabbit used the thorns and briers to escape, outsmarting the more powerful Fox with only his wits. Br'er Rabbit, like all tricksters, succeeds by tricking his oppressor into giving him what he wants. It was easy to see how a slave, who had no power and who was living in fear, could see "tricking" was a crafty and safe way of having power over the master.

However, the Shulammite never tricks and never schemes. Doc had taught his congregation that while those trickster stories were entertaining, followers of Jesus were to model their behavior after the integrous Shulammite, not the manipulative Br'er Rabbit!

"My goodness! Doc held his congregants to tough standards," I declared.

"Yes he did. No one minded. They knew Doc loved them no matter what."

I had lost count of how many times Caleb, Reggie, and I had met. But every meeting had been, for me, a holy experience. I wasn't sure why God had led Caleb to me, but I was thrilled for every moment I had had with both of these men.

Our last meeting took place on a beautiful spring day and we decided to walk along the National Mall. It seemed appropriate somehow. Caleb

---

giving her the freedom to leave the harem.

14. The Br'er Rabbit story was originally published in Harper's Weekly by Robert Roosevelt; years later Joel Chandler Harris included his version of the tale in his Uncle Remus stories. However, its origins can be traced back to an oral tradition perhaps passed from Cherokee Natives to African-American slaves in the early 1800s.

would walk for a while and then take a seat on a bench. Reggie and I would sit on either side of him and listen. We had almost reached the end of the story, but I still had questions. Caleb had a question too—his usual one.

"Give me your female take," he pried. Of course, he didn't have to pry hard.

"I think the Shulammite may have been the first feminist. Did you hear her say, 'My vineyard, my very own, is for myself?'[15] I hear her claiming her own voice, going up against the King and saying that she alone is "the boss of her." I love hearing confidence from this young black Middle Eastern peasant woman. Don't you imagine she could have been killed for that? She is going toe to toe with the King."

Reggie answered, "And she says it with such sass. She tells good old Solomon to keep the income of his vineyards and let his workers keep their income, but that no amount of money is going to buy her vineyard![16] She isn't afraid of him—at least not anymore."

"Why don't we teach this stuff to little girls?" I demanded.

"Because it dismantles sexism to teach little girls that they are in charge of their own bodies—or that rounded thighs and tummies are beautiful.[17] The oppressors want power over women," declared Reggie.

Perhaps because it was our last meeting, perhaps because it needed to be pointed out, I turned to Reggie, "You are good at this. Identify for me the oppressors in the unjust systems that keep women down."

"You know them." He pushed my elbow with the tips of his fingers, "You told us yourself that you stopped going to church because women didn't have leadership positions in your denomination."

"So the church is the oppressor of women?" I asked.

"One of many. More often than any of us would like to admit, organized religion is the oppressor. And not just to women. It denied slaves their freedom. Later it denied freed African-Americans their civil rights. However, oppressing a group of people is against the heart of the gospel—a gospel that teaches us that 'there is no longer Jew or Greek, there is no longer slave or free, there is no longer male and female; for all of you are one in Christ Jesus.'[18] Moreover, it teaches us to serve one another. You can't serve others when you aren't giving them the same freedoms and opportu-

15. Song 8:12.

16. Harper, *The Song of Solomon*, 61.

17. Song 7:1–2.

18. Gal 3:28.

nities you have. The true church never oppresses. Sexism is not a legitimate religious view any more than racism."

Caleb laughed—pleased with how Reggie was becoming so enthusiastic about the way of Jesus. The trees on the Mall were budding. The sky was crystal clear. It was such a contrast to the winter weather the day I had met Caleb. Together the three of us sat and contemplated life.

Reggie was the first to speak. "Have you noticed that not once in the Song was the Shulammite and the Shepherd's relationship based on the Shulammite following a list of rules, doing a set of good works, or buying into a certain theology? All that was required was saying yes to his invitation."

"I hadn't noticed. That is a good point." Then on another note, I asked Caleb, "Tell me how you went into politics?"

"I found that I enjoyed teaching political science. I was teaching high schoolers how they could use the American justice system to change the world. Then I started offering free lectures on Saturday morning, educating the adults in the community too. Just like how the villagers bring a young woman to the Shulammite for advice, my hometown was coming to me too. So I taught anyone who would listen."

Caleb taught at Harrelson another nine years when some of the men in Doc's church asked if they could run him for city council. He did that one term before a newly formed "Women of the NAACP" came around asking him to run for Congress.

"A women's group!" exclaimed Caleb. "I was so honored. They did their best and I did my best. I was elected to the House of Representatives in 1978 at the ripe old age of sixty-four. It's unheard of. I have been a shoo-in every election since."

"And today you are still listening, on behalf of the Good Shepherd, for those in need and interceding for them."

"I think *you* have listened well, young lady. It has been a joy to get to know you."

Caleb smiled and Reggie summed it all up with, "And that is how an old black man came to be a young Shulammite woman."

"Who you calling old?" Caleb mumbled as he stood and began lumbering his way back to his office. Reggie and I sat on the bench and laughed when after about thirty more steps, we could still hear Caleb. This time louder, "I'm not old!" And in another thirty feet more, he spun around and hollered back at Reggie, "I can still whoop *your* butt."

Those weeks I had spent with Congressman Morgan defined the rest of my life. We all live in the midst of unjust systems and oppressors of many kinds. I dare say that if we are not careful, we can even unwittingly become an oppressor.

Oppressors mock and trample on who we were created to be instead of nurturing and uplifting us. Unjust systems imprison us in "truths" that have been twisted into lies. Saying yes to the Good Shepherd is the first step in dismantling them. It will not be easy. It will not be straightforward, but we can lean on the Good Shepherd as we take that journey and we can support others on their journeys too.

We belong to the Good Shepherd and he belongs to us.

Epilogue

"Caleb!" I called excitedly into the basement rec room of our Arlington home, "It's time!!!"

"Coming Mom," answered my handsome second grader as he bounded up the stairs into the kitchen. He was dressed in suit and tie looking just as fine as his dad.

"Son, do you realize where we are going today?"

"To the inauguration of Barack Obama!" then with his little arms stretched out wide making a grand announcement to the world, "the first black president of the United States of America!"

"That's right!" laughed his dad, "This is a historic event that we will never forget!"

"That it is!" I declared as I kissed our son, who looked so much like his father except for the blue-green eyes. Yes, his father, my husband, was Reggie.

"Are we picking Congressman Caleb up?" asked young Caleb.

"Oh, the White House is sending a special car for Congressman Caleb. He gets to stand in a very special place during the inauguration." Congressman Caleb (as we had come to call Congressman Morgan since the birth of his namesake) was now ninety-five years old, long ago retired, and still fit as a fiddle. Reggie had worked as an advisor on the Obama campaign and would be an advisor in the President's cabinet. Hence, our invitation to a day of inauguration celebrations.

I still held down my job at the same DC think tank, which I had worked at now for more than seventeen years. My title was "Distinguished Fellow," which we all found humorous.

At the end of our last meeting, Caleb had left Reggie and me alone sitting on that bench on The Mall together. It was there that Reggie announced that he had decided he needed to dismantle the injustice his family was perpetuating against my white skin by taking me home to meet these "oppressors" whom he called mom and dad. Funny thing though, it turns out his fears that his family would be deeply hurt by his decision to date me were completely unfounded. They accepted and loved me like their own daughter. And I loved them too. My family took a bit longer to come around, but they did. It turns out that having a grandchild will soften almost any heart.

It just goes to show that the oppressor isn't always external to us. Sometimes we oppress ourselves and create our own unjust systems that keep us down. We let things get in our thoughts that keep us from being all God created us to be and having all that God meant for us to have. These internal unjust systems need to be dismantled too. Reggie had just needed a little time to come to terms with his.

Reggie and I were married a year later. Congressman Caleb was Reggie's best man. Not surprisingly, our vows ended with "I am my Beloved's, and he—or *she* in Reggie's case—is mine."

Prayer of Commitment

The Shulammite used the following words to commit herself fully to the Shepherd:

> "Set me as a seal upon your heart, as a seal upon your arm; for love is strong as death, passion fierce as the grave. Its flashes are flashes of fire, a raging flame. Many waters cannot quench love, neither can floods drown it. If one offered for love all the wealth of his house, it would be utterly scorned." (Song 8:6–7)

How to pray the Prayer of Commitment

If you so desire, write your commitment to the Good Shepherd. You can flip through the Song and find words that inspire your relationship to God. Borrow them if you would like. Or you can write your own. It need not be lyrical. It can be simple and to the point. Just make it a commitment to love the Shepherd with your whole heart.

Day 1–5

Start each day by sitting quietly and meditating on the Good Shepherd's love for you. Then work on your personal Prayer of Commitment. Write it, meditate on it, review it, change it, and pray it. Write it on a scrap of paper that you can take with you. Take it to the grocery store, to the office, to church—to anywhere you might go during the week. Open it up wherever you go and quietly pray it in all different situations. See how these different situations bring new thoughts and new meanings to your words. Journal.

Appendixes

Now as an elder myself and a witness of the sufferings of Christ, as well as one who shares in the glory to be revealed, I exhort the elders among you to tend the flock of God that is in your charge, exercising the oversight, not under compulsion but willingly, as God would have you do it—not for sordid gain but eagerly. Do not lord it over those in your charge, but be examples to the flock. And when the chief shepherd appears, you will win the crown of glory that never fades away.

—1 Peter 5:1–4

Lesson Plans for Study Groups

Study Introduction

This study guide has eight sessions. For group study, everyone will need their own copy of *Dismantling Injustice* and a journal to record reflections. Even though there are only eight lessons, you will want to carve out nine meeting sessions with the first meeting being a time to get to know each other and kick off the study.

Each lesson plan below has two sections: Preparation and Group Discussion.

The Preparation Section should be done prior to coming to the meeting. It will tell you which chapters to read and which Spiritual Practice to try throughout the week prior to class. Each Spiritual Practice will require that you carve out time daily over a five-day period. So if your meeting is on Sunday each week, then read the two required chapters on Monday so that you have Tuesday through Saturday to try each spiritual practice. How much time you carve out is up to you. Do not force yourself to spend a certain amount of time, but give yourself enough time to feel you have connected with God. Finding a place of stillness and quiet to practice these disciplines is extremely important. Some groups choose to meet every other week so that they have plenty of time to practice each discipline between classes.

The Group Discussion section is done together during the group meeting. Pick out the discussion questions that strike the most interest among the group and start with them. If the group gets interested in a certain topic, do not feel compelled to answer all of the questions each week.

Please note that Appendix 2 contains a Character List that readers may find helpful. Since the study group will be reading the book in weekly segments, it is easy to get the names of the characters confused between sessions. For this reason, some people like to read the book in total before starting the study. If you do this, be certain not to spoil future chapters for those who have not read them yet.

Pre-Study Meeting

Preparation:

The study leaders will want to make sure everyone has a book of their own and a journal before this meeting. The leaders should read the above Study Introduction and be prepared to share it with the group. Some groups like to rotate leadership; if this is the case, assign who will lead each lesson.

Group Discussion:

1. Introduce yourselves and share why you have joined this study.

2. Go over the Study Introduction above.

3. Ask everyone to commit to doing the Preparations and Spiritual Practices each week.

4. Ask everyone to commit to keeping conversations that go on within the study confidential.

Lesson 1—Relationship Assessment

Preparation:

Read The Meet Cute (chapters 1–2 and Spiritual Practice 1: The Relationship Assessment). Practice the Relationship Assessment as instructed in the reading.

Group Discussion:

1. How did the spiritual practice work out for you?

2. When have you felt the strongest connection to God? Why was your relationship strong during this time? Was there something you intentionally did?

3. When have you felt the weakest connection to God? Why was your relationship weak during this time? Was there something missing?

4. The quote at the beginning of chapter 1 says, "*Those who plan everything to a 'T' don't allow themselves to be surprised by the freshness, fantasy, and novelty of the Holy Spirit.*" The narrator calls the meeting between herself and Caleb "no happy accident." Caleb calls it a "divinely planned encounter." In addition, the Apostle Paul wrote, "For we are what God has made us, created in Christ Jesus for good works, which God prepared beforehand to be our way of life" (Eph 2:10). How often are you aware of God working this intimately in the events of your life? How can you become more aware of God's activity in your life?

Lesson 2—Lectio Divina

Preparation:

Read Conflicting Interpretations (chapters 3–4 and Spiritual Practice 2: Lectio Divina). Practice Lectio Divina as instructed in the reading.

Group Discussion:

1. How did the spiritual practice work out for you?

2. Pick one word, phrase, or idea that spoke to you during the week and share it with the group. What did the Holy Spirit reveal to you? How does it apply to your life? How can the group support you in what you have learned?

3. Did you enjoying practicing Lectio Divina? What were the positive points and what were the negative points? Share any tips you might have discovered.

4. Many people are not used to studying Scripture without a commentary or teacher. How did it feel to study it with the Holy Spirit as your only guide? Discuss Lectio Divina in light of the following verse where Jesus said, "But the Advocate, the Holy Spirit, whom the Father will send in my name, will teach you everything, and remind you of all that I have said to you" (Joh 14:26).

Lesson 3—Discerning Unjust Systems

Preparation:

Read Act 1: The Harem (chapters 5–6 and Spiritual Practice 3: Discerning Unjust Systems). Practice Discerning Unjust Systems as instructed in the reading.

Group Discussion:

1. How did the spiritual practice work out for you?

2. Name several unjust systems at work in your world. Who is the oppressor and who is the Harem that supports the oppressor? Is the Harem aware that they are enslaved and, by submitting to the oppressor, keeping the system going?

3. Have you ever been seduced by an unjust system thinking that it would provide something you wanted or needed? What was the outcome?

4. Have you ever been the oppressor? Consider this statement: "Shame [on] our dependence on the underpaid labor of others. When someone works for less pay than she can live on—when she goes hungry so that you can eat more cheaply and conveniently—then she has made a great sacrifice for you."[1] Does this resonate with you?

1. Barbara Ehrenreich, author of *Nickel and Dimed* (2010).

Lesson 4—Thankful Remembrance

Preparation:

Read Act 2: Solomon, the Oppressor (chapters 7–8 and Spiritual Practice 4: Eucharistic Remembrance). Practice Eucharistic Remembrance as instructed in the reading.

Group Discussion:

1. How did the spiritual practice work out for you?

2. Notice all the ways that Solomon flatters the Shulammite's looks. No doubt that she is physically beautiful or he wouldn't desire her. Nevertheless, when is flattery a good thing and when is it a tool of an unjust system that wants to enslave?

3. The saying "speak truth to power" is often used to describe when speaking out about injustice is appropriate. How does the Shulammite speak truth to the oppressor (Solomon)? How does the Shulammite speak truth to the victims of oppression (the Harem)? Can we fight injustice if the victims of injustice are so entranced by the oppressor that they do not think they need to be freed? Can you think of modern day examples where victims willingly supporting their oppressors simply because they are not well informed or educated on their options?

4. The Shulammite is reminded of the Shepherd by the smell from the perfume satchel around her neck. Caleb is reminded of the calling God had on his life by the deer head in Rufus's office. What things can you place around you that will remind you of God? Cross necklaces are beautiful, but it is similar to wearing a miniature electric chair around one's neck. Make a list of positive things that will remind you of God.

Lesson 5—Praying the Labyrinth

Preparation:

Read Act 3: The Good Shepherd (chapters 9–10 and Spiritual Practice 5: Praying the Labyrinth). Practice Praying the Labyrinth as instructed in the reading.

Group Discussion:

1. How did the spiritual practice work out for you?

2. God is as taken with you as the Good Shepherd is with the Shulammite. But are you in love with God? Are you ready to live into the love God feels for you? Reflect on Zep 3:17: "The LORD, your God, is in your midst, a warrior who gives victory; he will rejoice over you with gladness, he will renew you in his love; he will exult over you with loud singing."

3. The Shulammite uses covenant language when she says, "My beloved is mine and I am his." In Lev 26:12 God used covenant language with Moses, "I will walk among you, and will be your God, and you shall be my people." Have you made a covenant commitment to God? If not, what "little foxes" are holding you back? Hallie was trying to hold Caleb back from having a meaningful relationship with God. Do you have people or things in your life that hold you back?

4. Notice that the Good Shepherd never condemns the Shulammite for getting caught up in the unjust world system. He simply offers her a new life with him. How does this lack of condemnation work itself out in the life of Jesus? Hint: "For God so loved the world that he gave his only Son, so that everyone who believes in him may not perish but may have eternal life. Indeed, God did not send the Son into the world to condemn the world, but in order that the world might be saved through him" (Joh 3:16–17).

Lesson 6—Radical Prayer

Preparation:

Read Act 4: Love Triangle (chapters 11—12 and Spiritual Practice 6: Radical Prayer). Practice the Radical Prayer as instructed in the reading.

Group Discussion:

1. How did the spiritual practice work out for you?

2. When an unjust system or an oppressor thinks that they can buy you, they will try. This fact often puts us at risk of being manipulated into seeing unjust systems and the oppressor as desirable. What things does God offer us that are more desirable?

3. Go back to chapter 4 and reread Song 4:1-15. Note the contrasts between the way Solomon and the Shepherd romance the Shulammite. What is your reaction to the two men?

4. Jake has chosen a bad path—one that will hurt the woman he is having an affair with, his own family, and himself. Caleb explains that Jake is so entrenched in his family's unjust system that escaping from it is too much for him. Are there any unjust systems that you are so entrenched in that you can't imagine the radical changes it would require for you to get out of them or fix them?

Lesson 7—Seeking God in our Dreams

Preparation:

Read Act 5: The Shulammite's Nightmare (chapters 13—14 and Spiritual Practice 7: God in our Dreams). Practice God in our Dreams as instructed in the reading.

Group Discussion:

1. How did the spiritual practice work out for you?

2. Read the Parable of the Sower in Matthew 13:3–9. How many ways are unjust systems destroying our relationship with God in this parable? Can you relate them to your own life? How do you protect yourself from these unjust systems?

3. Think about a path that you have chosen to go down even though you knew that it wasn't the path God was leading you to go down. Why did you choose that path instead of the one God wanted you to choose? What was the outcome?

4. Hallie asked the question, "Where was your God when your dad was getting beat up?" Questions like this can tear us away from having a close relationship with God. How do you answer this question? How did Caleb answer it?

Lesson 8—Prayer of Commitment

Preparation:

Read Act 6: Love Wins (chapters 15—16, the epilogue, and Spiritual Practice 8: Prayer of Commitment). Write your Prayer of Commitment as instructed in the reading.

Group Discussion:

1. How did the spiritual practice work out for you?

2. The villagers say that looking on the Shulammite is like looking "upon a dance before two armies." How is this so? How was Caleb like a "dance between two armies?" How is every life lived following the Good Shepherd like a dance between two armies?

3. Caleb, like the Shulammite, used what God taught him from his missteps to teach others. Can you do this? What would hold you back?

4. Does responding to God as a person responds to his or her beloved feel appropriate to you? If not, why not? Why do you think this ancient opera, written about one thousand years before the birth of Christ, survived?

5. The last words of the Good Shepherd were, "O you who dwell in the gardens, my companions are listening for your voice; let me hear it" (Song 8:13). The last words of Jesus to his disciples were, "Go therefore and make disciples of all nations, baptizing them in the name of the Father and of the Son and of the Holy Spirit, and teaching them to obey everything that I have commanded you. And remember, I am with you always, to the end of the age" (Mat 28:19–20). How are these last words both alike and different? How do they affect the way you live? Hint: See footnote 12 in chapter 16.

APPENDIX 2

Character List

Main Characters and Locales in the Parable

Congressional Representative Caleb Morgan—African-American athlete who grew up in Harrelson, Georgia. He was adopted by Doc Morgan and his wife as a young boy. Congressman Morgan had a professional football career until he cracked a vertebra, at which time he returned to Harrelson as a coach. Then he later took a coaching job at an all-white school in Grandville, Georgia.

Doc Morgan—Caleb's adopted father. The nickname "Doc" was given after Doc Morgan received his PhD in Theology. He is the African-American minister in Colquitt County, Georgia where Harrelson is located.

Grandville—A town in middle Georgia located in Carroll County. Rufus and the rest of the Bennett clan lives here. Caleb takes a coaching job here.

Hallie Bennett—The promiscuous daughter-in-law of Rufus Bennett and wife of Jake Bennett. She grew up on the wrong side of the tracks and married Jake for his money.

Harrelson—South Georgia town where Caleb grew up and returned as a coach. It is where Doc Morgan lives.

Jake Bennett—Son of Rufus Bennett and husband of Hallie Bennett.

Reggie—Assistant to Congressional Representative Caleb Morgan.

Rufus Bennett—Patriarch of the Bennett clan. Everyone knows that he runs Grandville.

Wade—Malevolent son-in-law of Rufus Bennett. He is a thug.

Main Characters and Locales in the Song of Solomon

Eunuchs—The castrated soldiers who guard the King's harem.

Girl—A young girl from the village of Shulem who is brought to the Shulammite for advice at the very end of the Song.

Harem—Wives and concubines of King Solomon sometimes called Daughters of Jerusalem.

Jerusalem—The holy city of Israel where King Solomon has built the temple and where he has a palace.

King Solomon –The lustful King of Israel and adult son of King David.

Shepherd—A lowly male peasant from the city of Shulem who loves the Shulammite.

Shulammite—A young peasant woman from the city of Shulem.

Shulem—The village where the Shulammite is from. It is located in the Northern Kingdom near Lebanon. King Solomon has a country estate nearby.

Villagers—The villagers from Shulem.

Bibliography

Assis, Elie. *Flashes of Fire: A Literary Analysis of the Song of Songs.* The Library of Hebrew Bible/Old Testament Studies. New York: Bloomsbury T&T Clark, 2009.

Brenner, Athalya, and Carole R. Fontaine, eds. *The Song of Songs.* The Feminist Companion to the Bible. Wiltshire, Great Britain: Sheffield Academic, 2000.

Brichto, Sidney. *Song of Songs.* London: Sinclair-Stevenson, 2000.

Bullock, C. Hassell. *An Introduction to the Old Testament Poetic Books.* Chicago: Moody, 1988.

Carr, Lloyd G. *The Song of Solomon: An Introduction and Commentary.* Tyndale Old Testament Commentaries 19. Downers Grove, Illinois: IVP Academic, 1984.

Clarke, Elizabeth. *Politics, Religion and the Song of Songs in Seventeenth-Century England.* Hampshire, England: Palgrave Macmillian, 2011.

Coleman, Caryl. "Birds (In Symbolism)." In *The Catholic Encyclopedia; Volume 2,* New York: Robert Appleton, 1913.

Copan, Paul. *Is God a Moral Monster? Making Sense of the Old Testament God.* Grand Rapids, Michigan: Baker, 2011.

Cornelius, Izak, and John Hilber. *The Minor Prophets, Job, Psalms, Proverbs, Ecclesiastes, Song of Songs.* Zondervan Illustrated Bible Backgrounds Commentary 5. Grand Rapids, Michigan: Zondervan, 2009.

Driver, S. R. *An Introduction to the Literature of the Old Testament.* Edinburgh: T. & T. Clark, 1913.

Elliot, Mark W. *The Song of Songs and Christology in the Early Church.* Eugene, Oregon: Wipf & Stock, 2011.

Exum, J. Cheryl. *Song of Songs: A Commentary.* The Old Testament Library. Louisville: Westminster John Knox, 2005.

Falk, Marcia. *The Song of Songs: A New Translation and Interpretation.* New York: HarperCollins, 1993.

———. *The Song of Songs: Love Lyrics from the Bible.* HBI Series on Jewish Women. Lebanon, New Hampshire: Brandeis University Press, 2004.

Fletcher, Elizabeth Jane. *Women in the Bible: A Historical Approach.* New York: Harper Collins, 1997.

Garrett, Duane A. *Ecclesiastes, Song of Solomon.* Shepherd's Notes. Nashville: Holman Reference, 1998.

Ginsburg, Christian D. *The Song of Songs: Translated from the Original Hebrew with a Commentary, Historical and Critical.* Eugene, Oregon: Wipf and Stock, 2009.

Glendhill, Tom. *The Message of the Song of Songs.* Downers Grove, Illinois: IVP, 1994.

BIBLIOGRAPHY

Glickman, S. Craig. *A Song for Lovers*. Downers Grove, Illinois: IVP, 1976.

Godet, F. "The Interpretation of the Song of Songs" in *Studies in the Old Testament*, 241–90. New York: Hodder and Stoughton, 1894.

Guyon, Jeanne. *Song of Songs of Solomon: Explanations and Reflections Having Reference to the Interior Life*. Charleston, South Carolina: Nabu, 2011.

———. *Song of the Bride*. New Kensington, Pennsylvania: Whitaker, 1997.

Hamilton, Virginia. *The People Could Fly: American Black Folktales*. New York: Knopf, 1985.

Harper, Andrew. *The Song of Solomon*. The Cambridge Bible for Schools and Colleges. Cambridge: University Press, 1902.

Hill, Andrew E. "The Song of Solomon." In *The Evangelical Commentary on the Bible*, edited by Walter A. Elwell, 452–66. Grand Rapids: Baker, 1989.

Horine, Steven C. *Interpretive Images in the Song of Songs: From Wedding Chariots to Bridal Chambers*. New York: Peter Land, 2001.

Jenson, Robert W. *Song of Songs*. Interpretation Series. Louisville: John Knox, 2005.

Johnson, Frank. *Proverbs, Ecclesiastes, and Song of Solomon*. Basic Bible Commentary 11. Nashville: Abingdon, 1988.

Kaiser, Walter C., ed. *Classical Evangelical Essays in Old Testament Interpretation*. Grand Rapids, Michigan: Baker, 1972.

Kauk, Myron C. "Song of Solomon: A Defense of the Three Character Interpretation." Paper presented to the 55th Meeting of the Midwest Region of the Evangelical Theological Society. St Paul, Minnesota, March 19–20, 2010. https://myronkauk.files.wordpress.com/2009/06/song-of-solomon-defense-of-three-character-interpretation.pdf.

Kreeft, Peter. *Three Philosophies of Life: Song of Songs: Life as Love*. San Francisco: Ignatius, 1989.

Longman III, Tremper. *Song of Songs*. Grand Rapids: Eerdmans, 2001.

Malaty, Tadrous Y. *The Song of Songs*. A Patristic Commentary. Translated by Ferial Moawad. Sporting-Alexandria, Egypt: George's Coptic Orthodox Church, 2005. http://www.orthodoxebooks.org/sites/default/files/pdfs/Song%20of%20Songs%20-%20Father%20Tadros%20Yacoub%20Malaty.pdf.

Morrison, Toni. *Song of Solomon*. New York: Alfred A. Knopf, 1977.

Norris Jr., Richard A. *The Song of Songs: Interpreted by Early Christian and Medieval Commentators*. The Church's Bible 1. Grand Rapids, Michigan: Eerdmans, 2003.

Pope, Marvin H. *Song of Songs: A New Translation with Introduction and Commentary*. The Anchor Bible. Garden City, New York: Double Day, 1977.

Provan, Iain. *Ecclesiastes, Song of Songs*. The New Application Commentary. Grand Rapids, Michigan: Zondervan, 2001.

Rothstein, J. W. "The Song of Songs." In *Dictionary of the Bible Dealing with its Language, Literature, and Contents Including the Biblical Theology*. Vol 4, 589–97. New York: Charles Scribner's Sons, 1902. http://www.ccel.org/ccel/hastings/dictv4/Page_589.html.

Smith, Malcolm. "Song of Solomon." Lecture on CD. Bandera, Texas: Unconditional Love International, MP3 file.

Soughers, Tara. *Falling in Love with God: Passion, Prayer, and the Song of Songs*. Cambridge, Massachusetts: Cowley, 2005.

Stockett, Kathryn. *The Help*. New York: G.P. Putnam's Sons, 2009.

Swanson, Kenneth. "Essays on Spiritual Direction." Unpublished Essays. Roswell, Georgia: St. David's Episcopal Church, 2014.

Tournay, Raymond Jacques. *Word of God, Song of Love: A Commentary on the Song of Songs*. New York: Paulist, 1988.

Walton, John, et al., *The IVP Bible Background Commentary: Old Testament*. Downers Grove, Illinois: IVP, 2008.

Waterman, Leroy. *The Song of Songs*. Ann Arbor: University of Michigan Press, 1948

Wright, J. Robert. *Proverbs, Ecclesiastes, Song of Solomon*. Ancient Christian Commentary on Scripture. Downers Grove, Illinois: IVP, 2005.